I0003849

OpenAI Agents SDK

A Hands-On Guide to Building Autonomous Agents with
OpenAI's Language Models

Morgan Devline

©

First Edition – 2025

Table of Content

Chapter 1: Introduction to OpenAI Agents SDK

1.1 What are Autonomous AI Agents?

Autonomous AI agents are software applications powered by artificial intelligence, capable of independently performing tasks, making decisions, and interacting with external systems without continuous human supervision. Think of them as intelligent assistants that not only follow instructions but can also proactively adapt their behavior based on changing circumstances or new information.

For example, an autonomous customer-support agent can independently handle customer queries, troubleshoot problems, and even escalate complex issues to human experts automatically, saving significant human resources and improving customer satisfaction.

1.2 of OpenAI Agents SDK

The **OpenAI Agents SDK** is a developer-friendly toolkit provided by OpenAI to build sophisticated, autonomous agents leveraging powerful OpenAI language models (such as GPT-4 Turbo and GPT-4o). The SDK simplifies the creation, deployment, and scaling of agents that autonomously plan, reason, and execute tasks using natural language prompts and structured workflows.

At its core, the SDK provides:

- **Easy integration with OpenAI's advanced language models**
- **Pre-built abstractions for agent behaviors** (e.g., task planning, tool integration, memory management)
- **Extensible architecture for custom integrations** (databases, external APIs, productivity tools)
- **Scalable deployment solutions**

The SDK empowers developers to shift their focus from low-level implementation details toward designing high-value agent behaviors and real-world business solutions.

1.3 Key Features and Capabilities

The OpenAI Agents SDK is designed for practicality and ease of use. Its key capabilities include:

Feature	Description and Benefit
Agent Planning and Reasoning	Automatic task decomposition and planning
Integration Flexibility	Seamless connectivity with third-party APIs and databases
Context and Memory Management	Persistent context awareness and long-term memory
Robust Error Handling	Built-in mechanisms for graceful error recovery
Customizable Workflows	Modular, reusable task sequences for efficiency
Optimized Performance	Tools for managing cost, token usage, and latency

These features make it straightforward to build advanced autonomous systems that solve practical industry problems.

1.4 Real-world Applications

OpenAI agents are already transforming various industries through tangible use cases:

- **Customer Support:** Autonomous agents reduce response time and cost, handling common issues 24/7.
- **Data Analytics:** Agents autonomously extract insights from data sources and generate real-time reports.
- **Marketing Automation:** Automated generation of personalized campaigns, social media posts, and email sequences.

- **Finance and Investments:** AI-driven decision-making for portfolio optimization, market research, and risk management.
- **Content Creation:** Autonomous writing and content generation, adapting dynamically to user preferences.

Each of these applications illustrates the SDK's power and flexibility, clearly aligning with real-world business needs and challenges.

1.5 Audience and Prerequisites

This book is intended for software developers, engineers, data scientists, AI practitioners, and technology leaders who wish to leverage OpenAI's powerful language models to build practical, autonomous AI agents.

Recommended Prerequisites:

- Familiarity with Python programming (intermediate level)
- Basic understanding of APIs, cloud computing, and databases
- Fundamental knowledge of artificial intelligence and NLP (natural language processing) concepts
- However, step-by-step tutorials, clear explanations, and practical projects throughout this book will guide even newcomers in successfully mastering the SDK.

1.6 How to Use This Book Effectively

To maximize your learning experience, follow these recommendations:

- **Sequential Approach:** Start with foundational chapters (1-3) to clearly grasp the basics, then move progressively into advanced chapters.
- **Practical Implementation:** Engage directly with provided code examples, run them, and experiment independently.
- **Hands-on Projects:** Complete real-world projects and exercises in each chapter to consolidate your understanding.
- **Use Visual Aids:** Refer frequently to tables, diagrams, and flowcharts for visual clarity on complex topics.
- **Continuous Learning:** Regularly refer to the appendices and recommended resources for ongoing growth and expertise.

Following these guidelines ensures that you'll quickly become proficient at building robust and autonomous OpenAI-powered agents.

Chapter 2: Setting Up Your Development Environment

2.1 Installation and Requirements

Before creating your first OpenAI autonomous agent, you'll need to set up your development environment properly. This section provides clear, easy-to-follow instructions on installation and outlines essential system requirements.

System Requirements

Ensure your system meets these minimal requirements:

Component	Recommended Specifications
Operating System	Windows 10+, macOS 10.15+ (Catalina), or Linux
Python Version	Python 3.8 or higher (recommended Python 3.11)
CPU	Intel i5 or AMD Ryzen equivalent (or better)
RAM	Minimum 8 GB RAM (16 GB+ recommended)
Storage	5 GB available disk space
Internet	Reliable internet connection (for API access)

Step-by-Step Installation

Follow these clear steps to successfully install and configure the OpenAI Agents SDK:

Step 1: Install Python

Verify your Python version first by opening your terminal or command prompt and running:

```bash
python --version
```

If you don't have Python installed, download and install it from python.org. Use Python 3.11 if possible, as it's optimized for stability and performance.

Step 2: Set Up a Virtual Environment

Using a virtual environment is highly recommended to manage project dependencies cleanly:

On macOS/Linux:

bash

```
python -m venv openai_agents_env
source openai_agents_env/bin/activate
```

On Windows:

bash

```
python -m venv openai_agents_env
.\openai_agents_env\Scripts\activate
```

You should now see the name of your environment (openai_agents_env) at the start of your command line.

Step 3: Install the OpenAI Package

Install the latest OpenAI Python package, which includes support for OpenAI's API, tools, and the Agents SDK capabilities:

bash

```
pip install --upgrade openai
```

Confirm the installation by running:

bash

```
pip show openai
```

You should see detailed package information displayed clearly, confirming your successful installation.

Step 4: Obtain Your OpenAI API Key

An API key is required to interact with OpenAI services:

- Log in or sign up at <u>OpenAI platform</u>.
- Navigate to **API Keys** under your profile settings.

Click **Create new secret key**, and save your key securely—**never share or publish this key publicly**.

Step 5: Configure API Key Securely in Your Environment

To securely use your API key within your Python scripts:

macOS/Linux:

Open your terminal, and run:

```
bash
```

```
export OPENAI_API_KEY='your-api-key-here'
```

For convenience, you can add this line to your `~/.bashrc` or `~/.zshrc` file.

Windows:

Run in Command Prompt:

```
cmd
```

```
setx OPENAI_API_KEY "your-api-key-here"
```

Restart your command prompt or IDE afterward.

Testing Your Installation

Run this quick test to verify your installation and API setup. In your Python environment, create a new file `test_openai.py`:

python

```python
import openai
import os


openai.api_key = os.getenv("OPENAI_API_KEY")


# Test prompt
response = openai.ChatCompletion.create(
    model="gpt-3.5-turbo",
    messages=[{"role": "user", "content": "Hello,
OpenAI!"}]
)


print(response.choices[0].message.content)
```

Run the script from your terminal:

bash

```bash
python test_openai.py
```

If correctly configured, the script will return a friendly greeting from OpenAI's model, like:

css

```
Hello! How can I assist you today?
```

Troubleshooting Common Installation Issues

If you encounter issues during installation or testing, use the following troubleshooting tips:

Issue	Solution
`ModuleNotFoundError: No module named 'openai'`	Confirm your virtual environment is activated and reinstall using `pip install openai`.
`AuthenticationError`	Double-check your API key configuration and ensure no extra spaces are copied.
Network Errors	Ensure a stable internet connection and retry your request.

Now that your development environment is set up, you're fully prepared to start building autonomous OpenAI agents.

2.2 SDK Installation (Local and Cloud Environments)

In this section, you'll learn how to install the OpenAI Agents SDK both locally on your personal machine and on popular cloud environments like Google Colab or AWS. Clear, practical instructions ensure you have a smooth and successful setup experience.

Local Installation

Local installation provides full control and flexibility for developing, testing, and debugging your autonomous agents.

Step 1: Ensure Python Environment is Ready

If you haven't already, create and activate a Python virtual environment:

macOS/Linux:

bash

```
python -m venv openai_agents_env
source openai_agents_env/bin/activate
```

Windows:

bash

```
python -m venv openai_agents_env
.\openai_agents_env\Scripts\activate
```

Step 2: Install Required Dependencies

Run the following command in your activated virtual environment to install essential packages:

bash

```
pip install --upgrade openai python-dotenv
```

openai: Contains the OpenAI SDK and tools.

python-dotenv: Securely manage your environment variables (API keys).

Step 3: Verify Installation Locally

Test your installation by running a quick Python command in your terminal:

python

```
python -c "import openai;
print(openai.__version__)"
```

A successful installation outputs the installed SDK version (e.g., `1.13.3`), confirming everything is set.

Cloud Environment Installation

Cloud environments are ideal for quickly experimenting or collaborating without extensive local setup.

Below are detailed guides for two common platforms: **Google Colab** and **AWS (Amazon Web Services)**.

Option A: Google Colab

Google Colab provides free access to hosted Jupyter notebooks and Python environments.

Step-by-Step Installation:

1. Open a new notebook

Navigate to `https://colab.research.google.com/`

Create a new notebook (`File → New notebook`).

2. Install OpenAI SDK
In the notebook cell, type:

```
bash
```

```
!pip install --upgrade openai python-dotenv
```

Run the cell (`Shift + Enter`).

3. Set up API Key securely

Add a new cell and use this template:

```python
python
```

```python
import openai
import os


os.environ["OPENAI_API_KEY"] = "your-api-key-here"
openai.api_key = os.getenv("OPENAI_API_KEY")
```

Replace `"your-api-key-here"` with your own key obtained securely from OpenAI platform.

4. Verify the installation
Run another cell:

```python
python
```

```python
response = openai.ChatCompletion.create(
    model="gpt-3.5-turbo",
    messages=[{"role": "user", "content": "Hello
from Google Colab!"}]
)


print(response.choices[0].message.content)
```

If successful, you'll receive a clear AI-generated greeting.

Option B: AWS (Amazon EC2 Instance)

AWS offers powerful cloud computing resources ideal for scalable, secure agent deployment.

Step-by-Step Installation:

1. Launch EC2 instance:

Log in to your AWS Management Console.

Launch an EC2 instance (`t2.medium` recommended with Ubuntu 22.04 LTS AMI).

2. Connect via SSH to your EC2 instance:

bash

```
ssh -i "your-key-pair.pem" ubuntu@your-instance-public-ip
```

Replace `"your-key-pair.pem"` and `your-instance-public-ip` with your details.

3. Update system and install Python:

bash

```
sudo apt update && sudo apt upgrade -y
sudo apt install python3-pip python3-venv -y
```

4. Create a virtual environment and install OpenAI SDK:

bash

```
python3 -m venv openai_agents_env
source openai_agents_env/bin/activate
pip install --upgrade openai python-dotenv
```

5. Configure your API key securely:
Run the command:

bash

```
export OPENAI_API_KEY='your-api-key-here'
```

Add it permanently to your environment (optional):

```bash
bash
```

```bash
echo 'export OPENAI_API_KEY="your-api-key-here"' >>
~/.bashrc

source ~/.bashrc
```

6. Verify the installation:

Create `test_sdk.py` file on your instance using `nano test_sdk.py`:

```python
python
```

```python
import openai

import os


openai.api_key = os.getenv("OPENAI_API_KEY")


response = openai.ChatCompletion.create(
    model="gpt-3.5-turbo",
    messages=[{"role": "user", "content": "Hello
from AWS EC2!"}]
)


print(response.choices[0].message.content)
```

Run the script:

```bash
bash
```

```bash
python test_sdk.py
```

If installation is correct, you'll receive a clear AI-generated response.

Troubleshooting Installation Issues (Local and Cloud)

Issue	Solution
Missing Module (`openai`)	Reinstall dependencies (`pip install --upgrade openai`).
Authentication Error	Check API key correctness, environment variable setup, and permissions.
Network Errors (Timeout, DNS)	Verify your internet connectivity and firewall settings, especially on cloud platforms.
AWS SSH Connection Failures	Check EC2 instance security group inbound rules (port 22).

Summary and Next Steps

You've now learned how to install and verify the OpenAI Agents SDK in both local and cloud-based development environments.

2.3 API Keys and Authentication

To securely and effectively use the **OpenAI Agents SDK**, proper handling of API keys and authentication is essential. In this section, you'll learn exactly how to generate, secure, and configure your OpenAI API key for seamless integration.

What is an OpenAI API Key?

An **OpenAI API Key** is a secure token provided by OpenAI that authenticates your requests to OpenAI services. It's crucial to keep this key confidential, as it grants direct access to OpenAI resources linked to your account.

Step 1: Generating Your API Key

Follow these clear steps to obtain your API key from OpenAI:

- Visit the OpenAI Platform and log in with your account credentials.
- Click on your profile icon (top right corner) and select **"API Keys"**.
- Click **"Create new secret key"**.
- Copy your key immediately after creation—OpenAI displays it only once.

Important Security Note:

Never share your API key publicly or commit it into public repositories.

Store it securely using environment variables or dedicated secret management tools.

Step 2: Securely Storing Your API Key

Storing your API key securely is critical. The recommended way to store API keys securely for local development is by using environment variables via a .env file.

Method: Using .env (Recommended)

1. Install python-dotenv:

bash

```
pip install python-dotenv
```

2. Create a .env file in your project directory:

ini

```
OPENAI_API_KEY="your-api-key-here"
```

Replace "your-api-key-here" with your actual API key.

3. Secure your .env file:

Add .env to your .gitignore to prevent accidental commits:

bash

```
echo ".env" >> .gitignore
```

Step 3: Accessing Your API Key from Python

To securely load and access your API key within your Python scripts, use the following approach:

Example code snippet:

python

```
import openai
import os
from dotenv import load_dotenv

# Load API key securely from .env
load_dotenv()
openai.api_key = os.getenv("OPENAI_API_KEY")

# Verify API key loaded successfully
if openai.api_key is None:
    raise ValueError("OpenAI API key not found.
Please check your .env file.")
```

```
# Test call to confirm authentication works

response = openai.ChatCompletion.create(

    model="gpt-3.5-turbo",

    messages=[{"role": "user", "content":
"Confirming API key authentication."}]

)


print(response.choices[0].message.content)
```

Running this script confirms successful authentication if it returns a valid response.

Step 4: Secure API Key Management in Cloud Environments

When deploying to cloud environments, manage API keys securely with built-in secret management tools.

Examples:

Environment	Recommended Method
AWS EC2	Use AWS Systems Manager Parameter Store or AWS Secrets Manager
Google Colab	Directly set via environment variables (`os.environ`)
Azure	Azure Key Vault
Heroku	Heroku Config Vars

Step 5: Troubleshooting Authentication Issues

Encountering authentication-related issues is common. Here's expert-level troubleshooting advice:

Issue Type	Recommended Solution
Invalid API Key Error	Ensure no extra spaces, typos, or quotation marks in your `.env` file or environment variables.
Authentication Failure	Confirm that your API key has proper permissions (check OpenAI account usage limits and billing status).
API Rate Limit Errors	Verify your usage limits via OpenAI dashboard and reduce API request frequency.
Environment Variables Not Loading	Double-check your `.env` file location and ensure you're correctly loading via `load_dotenv()`.

API Key Security Best Practices

- **Never expose API keys publicly** (GitHub repos, code-sharing platforms).
- **Use environment variables or dedicated secrets management tools** in production.
- **Regularly rotate your API keys** if compromised or at regular intervals as best practice.
- **Restrict API access and permissions** based on least-privilege principles.

Summary & Next Steps

- You now know exactly how to:
- Generate your OpenAI API key securely.
- Configure secure authentication via environment variables locally and in cloud environments.
- Troubleshoot authentication issues effectively.
- Follow security best practices.

With API key authentication set up securely, you're ready to confidently create your first autonomous OpenAI agent.

2.4 Your First Autonomous Agent: A Simple Example

Now that your environment is set up and your API keys are securely configured, you're ready to build your first autonomous agent using OpenAI's SDK. This example provides a clear, step-by-step guide to creating an agent that autonomously responds to simple user queries.

Step 1: Creating Your Project Structure

Begin by creating a clean, structured project folder:

bash

```
mkdir first-autonomous-agent
cd first-autonomous-agent
```

Inside this folder, create a virtual environment and activate it:

bash

```
python -m venv env
source env/bin/activate    # macOS/Linux
.\env\Scripts\activate     # Windows
```

Install required packages:

bash

```
pip install openai python-dotenv
```

Create a .env file to securely store your OpenAI API key:

ini

```
OPENAI_API_KEY="your-api-key-here"
```

Ensure your `.gitignore` includes `.env`:

bash

```bash
echo ".env" >> .gitignore
```

Step 2: Writing Your First Autonomous Agent

Create a new Python file named `simple_agent.py`:

python

```python
import openai
import os
from dotenv import load_dotenv

# Load API key securely from environment variable
load_dotenv()
openai.api_key = os.getenv("OPENAI_API_KEY")

# Define a simple autonomous agent function
def autonomous_agent(user_query):
    response = openai.ChatCompletion.create(
        model="gpt-3.5-turbo",
        messages=[
            {"role": "system", "content": "You are an autonomous assistant that answers user questions clearly and concisely."},
            {"role": "user", "content": user_query}
```

```
        ],
        temperature=0.7,   # Adjusts creativity of
responses
        max_tokens=150     # Limits response length
    )
    return
response.choices[0].message.content.strip()


# Example usage of the agent
if __name__ == "__main__":
    query = input("Ask your autonomous agent a
question: ")
    agent_response = autonomous_agent(query)
    print(f"\nAgent Response: {agent_response}\n")
```

Step 3: Running Your Autonomous Agent

Execute your script from the terminal:

```bash
```

```
python simple_agent.py
```

You'll see a prompt:

```css
```

```
Ask your autonomous agent a question:
```

Try entering a practical query, such as:

```sql
```

```
What are some benefits of using autonomous AI
agents?
```

You'll immediately receive a clear, concise, autonomous response from your agent.

Example Output:

```
pgsql
```

```
Agent Response: Autonomous AI agents can
significantly reduce human workload, handle
repetitive tasks, increase efficiency, operate 24/7
without fatigue, enhance accuracy, and scale easily
to manage complex or large-scale processes.
```

Step 4: Understanding the Code (Detailed Explanation)

Here's a clear breakdown of your autonomous agent's structure:

Imports and API configuration:
Loads OpenAI's library and API keys securely from the `.env` file.

Agent function (`autonomous_agent`):
Sends a structured prompt to the GPT model using a clearly defined system role (`system`) and the user query (`user`).

`temperature=0.7` controls creativity (higher values mean more creative answers).

`max_tokens=150` ensures concise responses.

Main execution block:
Accepts user input via the terminal, queries the agent function, and displays the response clearly.

Step 5: Troubleshooting Common Issues

Here's expert-level advice if you encounter any issues:

Issue	Troubleshooting Advice
`AuthenticationError`	Ensure your API key is correctly loaded in `.env` file without extra spaces.
`RateLimitError`	Reduce the frequency of API calls or wait before retrying.
Unexpected or irrelevant responses	Refine your prompt clearly or adjust the `temperature` parameter lower for more focused results (e.g., `0.2`).

Step 6: Enhancing Your Autonomous Agent

Experiment further by:

- **Improving prompts:**
  Provide clearer instructions to your agent via the `system` message for more precise behavior.
- **Adding memory/context:**
  Store previous interactions in memory (covered in later chapters).
- **Integrating external APIs:**
  Expand capabilities (detailed in upcoming sections).

Summary & Next Steps

- Congratulations—you've just successfully built your first simple yet effective autonomous AI agent with OpenAI's SDK. You learned how to:
- Set up a basic autonomous agent.
- Securely integrate API authentication.
- Craft clear, concise prompts for reliable agent performance.

2.5 Troubleshooting Common Setup Issues

Even the most straightforward setup processes can sometimes encounter unexpected issues. This section provides detailed, step-by-step guidance to quickly identify and resolve common setup problems when working with OpenAI Agents SDK.

Issue 1: ModuleNotFoundError: No module named 'openai'

Cause:

The `openai` Python package isn't correctly installed or you're not using your virtual environment.

Solution:

Check your environment activation:

macOS/Linux:

bash

```
source env/bin/activate
```

Windows:

bash

```
.\env\Scripts\activate
```

Reinstall OpenAI SDK:

bash

```
pip install --upgrade openai
```

Verify installation:

bash

```
python -c "import openai;
print(openai.__version__)"
```

Issue 2: AuthenticationError (Invalid API Key)

Cause:
Your API key is missing, incorrect, or improperly loaded.

Solution:

Verify your .env file contains exactly:

```ini
OPENAI_API_KEY="your-api-key-here"
```

Load the key securely:

```python
from dotenv import load_dotenv
import os

load_dotenv()
api_key = os.getenv("OPENAI_API_KEY")

if api_key is None:
    raise ValueError("API key not loaded. Check your .env file.")
```

Confirm no extra spaces or incorrect characters in your key.

Issue 3: RateLimitError: Too Many Requests

Cause:
You've reached the API usage limit or exceeded rate limits.

Solution:

Wait briefly (20-60 seconds) and retry your request.

Check API usage limits in your OpenAI dashboard.

Adjust frequency or batch your requests.

Issue 4: Permission Denied (File or Directory Access)

Cause:
Incorrect permissions or attempting installation in protected directories.

Solution:

Avoid installing packages globally with `sudo`.

Use virtual environments in user-level directories (`~/projects/your-project`).

Example:

bash

```
mkdir ~/openai-agent
cd ~/openai-agent
python -m venv env
source env/bin/activate
pip install openai
```

Issue 5: Python Version Compatibility Issues

Cause:
Using outdated Python versions not fully compatible with SDK.

Solution:

Verify Python version (`3.8` or above recommended):

bash

```
python --version
```

Upgrade to the latest Python version (ideally 3.11) from python.org.

Recreate your virtual environment:

```
bash
```

```
python -m venv env
source env/bin/activate
pip install --upgrade openai
```

Issue 6: Connection Errors (Timeout, DNS issues)

Cause:
Network connectivity problems, firewall blocking, or DNS issues.

Solution:

Check your internet connection and firewall settings.

Try simple connectivity tests (ping OpenAI):

```
bash
```

```
ping api.openai.com
```

Ensure your network isn't blocking API endpoints (api.openai.com).

Issue 7: OpenAI API Response Slow or Unresponsive

Cause:
High latency, model overload, or network latency.

Solution:

Use smaller or faster models (e.g., GPT-3.5-turbo instead of GPT-4) if applicable.

Reduce the `max_tokens` parameter or request complexity.

Monitor OpenAI Status Page for issues.

Expert Troubleshooting Checklist

Use this checklist to quickly identify setup issues:

Task	Action to Perform
Environment activated?	Run `source env/bin/activate` or `.env\Scripts\activate`
Packages correctly installed?	Verify via `pip freeze` or `pip show openai`
API key correctly configured?	Confirm `.env` file loading via `load_dotenv()`
API usage limit or rate limits exceeded?	Review OpenAI platform dashboard
Network issues?	Verify stable internet connectivity
Version compatibility (Python/OpenAI package)?	Use latest recommended versions

---

Troubleshooting Resources and Tips

Official Documentation: platform.openai.com/docs

Community Forums: community.openai.com

Check the SDK GitHub: github.com/openai/openai-python

When All Else Fails

If you continue experiencing persistent issues after these steps:

Fully reinstall SDK:

```bash
bash
```

```bash
pip uninstall openai

pip install --upgrade openai
```

Rebuild your environment: Delete and recreate virtual environments cleanly.

Seek community help: Post clearly defined questions on Stack Overflow or OpenAI community forums.

Chapter 3: Core Concepts and Architecture

3.1 Anatomy of an OpenAI Agent

To effectively build and deploy autonomous agents using the OpenAI SDK, it's essential to understand the fundamental components—or **anatomy**—of these agents. This section provides a clear breakdown of each core component, explaining its role with practical examples and real-world relevance.

What is an OpenAI Agent?

An **OpenAI agent** is an intelligent system powered by OpenAI's language models (like GPT-4 Turbo or GPT-4o), capable of independently performing complex tasks. These agents can understand user instructions, reason through tasks, interact with external systems, and autonomously generate solutions.

Think of an OpenAI agent as a highly skilled, AI-driven assistant capable of independently executing tasks and adapting dynamically to new information or contexts.

Core Components of an OpenAI Agent

Every OpenAI agent you build typically includes these five key components:

Component	Role & Description
Language Model	Core reasoning engine (e.g., GPT-4 Turbo) that generates intelligent responses.
Agent Prompt	Clearly instructs the model on its role, behavior, and goals.
Tools Integration	Enables interaction with external APIs, databases, or utilities.
Memory Management	Maintains context, remembering past interactions and decisions.

Component	Role & Description
Action and Execution Loop	Controls the autonomous behavior and decision-making processes, allowing agents to execute multiple steps independently.

Below is a detailed, practical breakdown of each component:

1. Language Model

The language model acts as the "brain" of your agent:

Examples: GPT-4o, GPT-4 Turbo, GPT-3.5 Turbo

Function: Performs reasoning, generates responses, plans tasks, and understands natural language instructions.

Real-world relevance:
Enables agents to adapt responses based on context, dynamically reason through tasks, and provide solutions autonomously.

2. Agent Prompt

The agent prompt sets clear expectations for your agent's behavior and role:

Example agent prompt:

```python
```

```
system_prompt = """

You are an autonomous customer support agent for a
SaaS product.

Always respond clearly, politely, and concisely.

If you cannot solve a customer's issue, escalate
immediately.

"""
```

Function: Clearly instructs the agent about its role, context, and acceptable behaviors.

Practical tip: Effective prompts are clear, concise, and define behavior explicitly to ensure predictable outcomes.

---

3. Tools Integration

Agents often interact with external systems to expand their capabilities significantly:

Examples: Web APIs (REST, GraphQL), databases (SQL, NoSQL), productivity tools (Slack, email, calendar).

Practical scenario:
A marketing agent autonomously sending campaign emails via Mailchimp API or fetching analytics from Google Analytics API.

Simple Example (pseudo-code integration):

```python
python


def fetch_user_data(user_id):
    response =
requests.get(f"https://api.yourapp.com/users/{user_id}")

    return response.json()


# Agent leveraging external API

user_info = fetch_user_data("user_12345")
```

---

4. Memory Management

Memory enables agents to retain context between interactions, critical for sophisticated tasks:

Memory Type	Use Case Example
Short-term	Storing recent conversation context for immediate tasks.
Long-term	Maintaining user preferences, historical decisions, and persistent knowledge.

Practical example:

```python
conversation_history = []

def add_to_memory(user_message, agent_response):
    conversation_history.append({"user": user_message, "agent": agent_response})

def get_memory():
    return conversation_history[-5:]  # Retrieves the last five interactions
```

This simple approach maintains conversational context effectively.

5. Action and Execution Loop

The execution loop allows the agent to autonomously perform multi-step tasks by sequentially making decisions, performing actions, and adapting to outcomes:

Practical Example (high-level concept):

```python
while not task_completed:
```

```
    action =
agent_decide_next_action(current_context)

    result = agent_execute_action(action)

    agent_update_context(result)
```

- **Real-world example:**
  An autonomous content-generation agent might:
- Generate an article outline.
- Write and review each section autonomously.
- Publish the content via an integrated CMS API.

Visualizing Agent Anatomy (Simple Diagram)

To clarify understanding, here's a simple table clearly summarizing agent anatomy:

Component	Function	Real-world Example
Language Model	Reasoning, understanding, decision-making	GPT-4 Turbo, GPT-4o
Agent Prompt	Clearly defined role, task clarity	Customer-support scenario prompt
Tools Integration	Interaction with external services	REST API for customer data
Memory Management	Context retention, personalization	Short-term conversation memory
Execution Loop	Autonomous multi-step task handling	Automated marketing campaign

---

Importance of Clearly Defining Agent Components

Clearly defining each component ensures:

- Reliable agent performance
- Predictable outcomes and behavior

- Efficient debugging and optimization
- Scalable development for complex real-world tasks

3.2 Understanding Agent Lifecycle

To effectively design, build, and deploy autonomous agents using the OpenAI SDK, you must clearly understand the agent lifecycle. The **agent lifecycle** represents the distinct stages an autonomous agent goes through—from initial task definition to completion and evaluation.

This section explains each lifecycle stage practically, illustrating how an agent moves through its decision-making and execution phases in real-world scenarios.

The Four Stages of the OpenAI Agent Lifecycle

An OpenAI autonomous agent typically follows these four clear stages:

Stage	Description
1. Initialization	Agent receives clear instructions and context.
2. Planning	Agent autonomously develops an execution plan.
3. Execution	Agent performs actions based on its plan.
4. Completion and Evaluation	Agent completes task, evaluates results, and adapts if necessary.

Let's explore each lifecycle stage practically, step-by-step.

Stage 1: Initialization

During initialization, the agent receives initial instructions (prompts), goals, and context. This initial stage is critical as it sets the foundation for how the agent behaves throughout its task.

Practical example: Initialization Prompt

```python
python
```

41

```
system_prompt = """
```

You are an autonomous customer support agent. Your task is to solve user issues quickly and politely.

If unable to resolve an issue, escalate clearly and immediately.

```
"""
```

What happens here:

Clearly defines the agent's role and responsibilities.

Provides foundational context and boundaries for behavior.

Stage 2: Planning

In the planning stage, your agent autonomously creates a clear, actionable plan or outline for completing its tasks based on the instructions provided. This involves the agent breaking down tasks into smaller, achievable subtasks.

Practical example (Conceptual Planning Process):

python

```
def agent_plan(task_description):
    prompt = f"""
    Your task is: {task_description}.

    Provide a step-by-step plan to accomplish this
task clearly and concisely.
    """
    response = openai.ChatCompletion.create(
        model="gpt-4o",
```

```
        messages=[{"role": "system", "content":
prompt}]
    )
    return response.choices[0].message.content
```

Example planning output:

```
markdown
```

1. Greet customer politely.

2. Identify the issue clearly.

3. Provide a step-by-step solution.

4. Verify the issue is resolved.

5. Close the conversation politely.

This ensures the agent has a structured approach before performing actions.

Stage 3: Execution

In this stage, the agent performs the actual steps or actions defined in the planning stage. This can involve interacting with external APIs, performing computations, generating content, or communicating with users.

Practical example (simplified execution loop):

```python
execution_plan = ["Greet customer", "Identify
issue", "Provide solution", "Verify solution",
"Close conversation"]


for step in execution_plan:
    action_prompt = f"Execute this step clearly:
{step}"
```

```python
    response = openai.ChatCompletion.create(
        model="gpt-4o",
        messages=[{"role": "system", "content":
action_prompt}]
    )
    action_result =
response.choices[0].message.content
    print(f"Action performed: {action_result}")
```

During execution:

Agent follows each step sequentially.

Clearly logs or returns results of each action for evaluation.

Stage 4: Completion and Evaluation

Upon completion, the agent evaluates the effectiveness of its actions. It may provide feedback, request additional clarification, or adjust its future behavior based on outcomes.

Practical example (evaluation step):

```python
python


evaluation_prompt = """

You've completed the customer support session.
Evaluate clearly whether the issue was resolved.

If unresolved, explain why clearly and suggest
escalation.

"""

evaluation_response = openai.ChatCompletion.create(
    model="gpt-4o",
```

```
    messages=[{"role": "system", "content":
evaluation_prompt}]

)
```

```
evaluation_result =
evaluation_response.choices[0].message.content
```

```
print(f"Evaluation: {evaluation_result}")
```

Example output:

```yaml
```

```
Evaluation: The issue was successfully resolved.
The customer confirmed the solution provided was
effective. No escalation required.
```

If evaluation indicates failure or incomplete resolution, the agent may escalate clearly or adjust future actions accordingly.

Real-world Lifecycle Example

Here's a clear practical example illustrating a complete lifecycle for an autonomous **customer support agent**:

Lifecycle Stage	Real-world Action Example
Initialization	Receives clear instructions on providing tech support.
Planning	Develops a step-by-step troubleshooting plan.
Execution	Greets customer, diagnoses problem, provides solution.
Completion & Evaluation	Confirms issue resolution, documents clearly, escalates if necessary.

Troubleshooting Common Lifecycle Issues

Here's practical advice for common issues encountered during an agent's lifecycle:

Issue	Expert-level Troubleshooting Advice
Incomplete Agent Plans	Refine your prompts to clearly request detailed, explicit planning.
Agent not Following Steps	Ensure structured, clearly numbered steps in your planning prompt.
Poor Agent Evaluation	Clearly instruct the agent to explicitly verify completion criteria during evaluation.

Best Practices for Managing the Agent Lifecycle

Follow these practical best practices to ensure smooth and reliable lifecycle management:

- **Clearly define agent roles** at initialization.
- **Keep prompts concise yet detailed** enough for clarity.
- **Use explicit step-by-step instructions** during the planning stage.
- **Implement clear evaluation criteria** to measure successful completion.
- **Regularly monitor agent outputs** and adapt prompts as necessary.

3.3 Selecting and Using Language Models (GPT-4o, GPT-4 Turbo)

Choosing the appropriate language model for your autonomous agent is crucial for optimal performance, efficiency, and cost-effectiveness. This section clearly explains the differences between the leading OpenAI language models (**GPT-4o and GPT-4 Turbo**), providing practical guidelines to help you select and effectively use the best model for your specific tasks.

of Key OpenAI Language Models

The two primary models used for building robust autonomous agents are:

Model	Strengths & Features	Ideal Use Cases
GPT-4o	High reasoning accuracy, multimodal, versatile, very fast inference.	Complex reasoning, real-time interactions, multimodal agents
GPT-4 Turbo	Highly capable, efficient, cost-effective, fast responses.	General-purpose tasks, customer support, chatbots, efficient large-scale deployments

Each model excels in different scenarios, making your selection highly practical based on project requirements.

---

1. GPT-4o: Advanced, Fast, and Multimodal

GPT-4o combines speed, versatility, and powerful reasoning abilities. It excels in complex scenarios and tasks requiring rapid, accurate decision-making.

Advantages:

- Exceptional reasoning accuracy.
- Faster inference speed than standard GPT-4.
- Multimodal capabilities (text, image understanding).
- High performance across diverse tasks.

Ideal Use Cases:

- Real-time autonomous agent interactions.
- Complex problem-solving and reasoning tasks.
- Multimodal interactions (handling images, text simultaneously).
- Situations demanding quick yet highly accurate responses.

Practical Example of GPT-4o Implementation:

```python
```

```python
import openai

response = openai.ChatCompletion.create(
    model="gpt-4o",
    messages=[
        {"role": "system", "content": "You are an
autonomous financial analyst agent. Analyze market
trends and provide concise summaries."},
        {"role": "user", "content": "Summarize
current trends in tech stocks."}
    ],
    temperature=0.5,
    max_tokens=200
)


print(response.choices[0].message.content.strip())
```

When to Prefer GPT-4o:

- Rapid and accurate decision-making required.
- Complex, multimodal interactions are necessary.
- Real-time performance is critical.

2. GPT-4 Turbo: Efficient and Cost-Effective

GPT-4 Turbo is optimized specifically for high efficiency, faster inference speeds, and lower operational costs, making it ideal for scalable deployments and general-purpose applications.

Advantages:

- Cost-effective compared to traditional GPT-4.
- Faster response time for efficient interactions.
- Reliable and versatile performance for most use cases.

- Ideal for large-scale applications.

Ideal Use Cases:

- Customer support agents with high-volume interactions.
- General-purpose autonomous tasks requiring speed and cost efficiency.
- Large-scale deployments or business scenarios with cost constraints.

Practical Example of GPT-4 Turbo Implementation:

python

```python
import openai

response = openai.ChatCompletion.create(
    model="gpt-4-turbo",
    messages=[
        {"role": "system", "content": "You are an autonomous customer service agent providing clear, concise support."},
        {"role": "user", "content": "How do I reset my password?"}
    ],
    temperature=0.2,
    max_tokens=100
)

print(response.choices[0].message.content.strip())
```

When to Prefer GPT-4 Turbo:

- Cost-sensitive scenarios.
- High-volume interactions with predictable responses.

- Efficient performance with less intensive reasoning tasks.

Comparative Practical Summary

Criteria	GPT-4o	GPT-4 Turbo
Reasoning Accuracy	Highest	High
Inference Speed	Fastest (among GPT-4 family)	Very Fast
Multimodal	Yes	No
Cost-effectiveness	Good (higher than Turbo)	Excellent (best economy)
Ideal for	Complex, multimodal, real-time scenarios	General-purpose, scalable, cost-sensitive scenarios

Use this practical summary to clearly inform your model selection process.

Best Practices for Choosing Models

Consider these practical best practices clearly:

- **Task complexity:**
  Choose GPT-4o for complex reasoning or multimodal needs; choose GPT-4 Turbo for more streamlined, repetitive tasks.
- **Budget constraints:**
  GPT-4 Turbo is cost-effective and ideal for scalable applications. Opt for GPT-4o when accuracy and speed are paramount and budget allows.
- **Performance vs. Cost trade-off:**
  Clearly evaluate the trade-off between performance needs (speed, accuracy, multimodal capabilities) and overall cost.
- **Testing and Iteration:**
  Practically test both models initially in your application scenario to measure performance, cost, and accuracy before committing fully.

Common Issues & Troubleshooting Model Usage

Here's practical advice for troubleshooting common issues when using these models:

Issue	Practical Troubleshooting Advice
Slow Responses (Latency)	Consider GPT-4o or GPT-4 Turbo for faster responses; reduce `max_tokens`.
High Costs	Shift to GPT-4 Turbo for routine tasks; optimize `max_tokens`.
Low Accuracy or Relevance	Refine your agent prompt clearly and reduce the `temperature`.

Summary & Next Steps

In this section, you've practically learned:

- Clear differences between GPT-4o and GPT-4 Turbo.
- Ideal scenarios for each model.
- Best practices for selecting the right model based on complexity, budget, and performance.
- Clearly understanding these differences enables you to choose and effectively utilize OpenAI models to maximize the performance, efficiency, and cost-effectiveness of your autonomous agents.

3.4 Essentials of Prompt Engineering for Agents

Prompt engineering is critical when designing and building autonomous agents with OpenAI's SDK. Effective prompts clearly define agent behavior, ensure accurate responses, and significantly improve task performance.

This section practically explains essential techniques, best practices, and real-world examples of prompt engineering specifically tailored for autonomous agents.

What is Prompt Engineering?

Prompt engineering involves carefully crafting instructions (prompts) that clearly guide AI models like GPT-4o or GPT-4 Turbo to produce desired outputs. In the context of autonomous agents, this means clearly specifying tasks, roles, contexts, behaviors, and expected responses.

Effective prompts lead directly to more accurate, reliable, and predictable agent behavior.

Key Principles of Effective Prompt Engineering

Successful prompt engineering for autonomous agents follows these practical principles:

- **Clarity**: Use explicit, straightforward instructions.
- **Specificity**: Clearly define tasks and agent roles precisely.
- **Conciseness**: Keep prompts brief yet comprehensive.
- **Contextualization**: Provide enough context for accurate understanding.
- **Structured formatting**: Organize prompts into clear, structured steps or numbered lists.

Practical Prompt Engineering Techniques

Here are practical techniques clearly demonstrated through real-world examples:

Technique 1: Clearly Defining Agent Role

Clearly defining the agent's role sets clear expectations:

Good Prompt Example:

```python
prompt = """
```

```
You are an autonomous travel planning assistant.
Your task is to create concise and personalized
travel itineraries based on user preferences.

"""
```

This clear, concise definition ensures accurate and consistent agent behavior.

Technique 2: Step-by-Step Instructions (Chain-of-Thought)

Break complex tasks down clearly into steps:

Example:

python

```
prompt = """

Your task is to book a flight clearly following
these steps:

1. Ask the user for their destination and preferred
travel dates.

2. Provide three best available flight options.

3. Clearly ask the user to select their preferred
flight.

4. Confirm the booking and provide booking details
clearly.

"""
```

Step-by-step instructions reduce mistakes and improve agent reliability.

Technique 3: Few-shot Prompting (Providing Examples)

Clearly include examples to guide agent responses accurately:

Example:

python

```
prompt = """
```

You're an autonomous product-review assistant.

Example:

Product: Wireless Earbuds

Review: "Clear sound quality, good battery life, comfortable fit."

Now write a clear, concise review for:

Product: Smartwatch

Review:

"""

Clearly providing examples helps guide the agent's response style accurately.

Technique 4: Limiting Responses with Constraints

Define explicit constraints clearly in the prompt for concise results:

Example:

python


```
prompt = """
```

You are an autonomous news summarizer agent. Summarize the following news article in exactly 3 sentences clearly and concisely:

[Article Text Here]

"""

Explicit constraints clearly control the length and style of the agent's output.

Technique 5: Providing Contextual Information

Include contextual details clearly to enhance relevance:

Example:

python

```
prompt = """
You are an autonomous customer support agent. Given
the following user history, respond clearly to the
user's current question.


User History:

- Purchased "Premium Subscription" last month

- Recently reported login issues


Current question: "I'm unable to access premium
features. Can you help?"


Your clear and concise response:
"""
```

Contextual information clearly increases the accuracy and relevance of the agent's replies.

Real-world Practical Prompt Examples

Here are practically tested, complete prompts used in real-world scenarios clearly demonstrating best practices:

Scenario	Prompt Example (Good Practice)
Customer Support	"You are an autonomous customer support agent. Resolve user issues clearly and escalate immediately if necessary."
Content Creation	"You're an autonomous content generation assistant. Clearly outline and write engaging articles based on provided topics."
Data Analyst Agent	"You are an autonomous data analyst. Clearly analyze the provided sales data and summarize key insights concisely."

Common Prompt Engineering Mistakes & Troubleshooting

Use this clear troubleshooting guide practically:

Issue	Practical Troubleshooting Advice
Vague or irrelevant responses	Clarify your prompts explicitly; use clear constraints.
Too lengthy or verbose answers	Clearly limit response length explicitly in your prompt (e.g., "in 2 sentences").
Agent misunderstanding tasks	Use clear, numbered step-by-step instructions in prompts.

Prompt Engineering Best Practices Checklist

Follow this clear, practical checklist consistently:

- Clearly define agent roles and tasks explicitly.
- Provide context and examples to guide responses.
- Include structured, step-by-step instructions.
- Explicitly limit response length and complexity.
- Continuously iterate and test prompts practically.

Summary & Next Steps

In this practical, detailed section, you've clearly learned essential prompt engineering techniques:

- Clearly defining agent roles
- Structured, step-by-step instructions
- Few-shot prompting with clear examples
- Explicit response constraints
- Contextualizing prompts clearly for accuracy
- Effective prompt engineering is a core skill, significantly enhancing your autonomous agents' accuracy, reliability, and performance.

3.5 Building Blocks of Agent Decision-making

To create effective and reliable autonomous agents, you must clearly understand how these agents make decisions. Autonomous agents built with OpenAI's SDK rely on several fundamental **building blocks** that enable them to analyze tasks, reason clearly, and execute actions confidently.

In this section, you'll practically learn about these building blocks and clearly see how they empower your agents to make accurate, intelligent, and autonomous decisions.

Core Building Blocks of Agent Decision-making

There are five core building blocks that clearly define an autonomous agent's decision-making process:

Building Block	Description
Context	Relevant background information influencing decisions.
Perception	Understanding inputs clearly and accurately.
Reasoning and Planning	Logical analysis and creating structured plans.

Building Block	Description
Decision and Action	Choosing optimal actions based on reasoning.
Feedback and Adaptation	Evaluating results and adapting future decisions.

Let's practically explore each of these building blocks in detail.

---

1. Context

Context represents essential background information or relevant data the agent clearly uses to make informed decisions.

Practical Examples:

Customer support:
Previous user interactions, purchase history, known user preferences.

Financial decision-making:
Historical market data, current economic indicators, portfolio status.

Clear Implementation Example:

python

```
context = {

    "user_history": ["Premium subscriber",
"Reported login issue previously"],

    "current_issue": "Unable to access premium
features"

}
```

Clear context enables the agent to respond accurately and relevantly.

---

2. Perception

Perception involves clearly and accurately interpreting inputs such as user queries, data, or external system responses.

Practical Examples:

Clearly understanding user intent from natural-language questions.

Extracting actionable insights from structured data.

Clear Example (Input Perception):

python

```
user_input = "What's the weather forecast tomorrow in London?"

agent_perception = {

    "intent": "weather_query",

    "location": "London",

    "time": "tomorrow"

}
```

Accurate perception significantly influences reliable decision-making.

---

3. Reasoning and Planning

Reasoning and planning involves logically analyzing tasks and creating structured, clear plans for execution.

Practical Examples:

Clearly outlining the steps for troubleshooting technical support issues.

Planning a series of investment actions based on market data analysis.

Clear Reasoning Example:

python

```
planning_prompt = """

You must resolve a customer's billing issue.
Provide a clear step-by-step reasoning plan.

"""
```

```
# Possible agent output:

# 1. Verify user's billing details.

# 2. Identify recent transactions clearly.

# 3. Determine discrepancies.

# 4. Provide clear resolution steps.
```

Effective reasoning ensures tasks are clearly structured, enhancing successful outcomes.

---

4. Decision and Action

Decision and action represent clearly selecting and executing the optimal actions based on reasoning outcomes.

Practical Examples:

Choosing clearly to escalate unresolved issues.

Clearly deciding the best investment option based on analysis.

Clear Example (Decision-making & Execution):

python

```python
def decide_and_act(plan):
    for step in plan:
        action_response = agent.execute(step)
        print(f"Executing step: {step}\nResult: {action_response}")
```

Accurate decision-making leads directly to effective agent outcomes.

5. Feedback and Adaptation

Feedback and adaptation involve evaluating agent actions and clearly adjusting future decisions based on past performance.

Practical Examples:

Learning from past incorrect responses to improve accuracy.

Adjusting agent behavior clearly based on user feedback.

Clear Example (Evaluation and Adaptation):

```python
feedback_prompt = """
Evaluate if the customer's issue was resolved.
Provide feedback clearly and suggest improvements
for future interactions.
"""


# Agent might respond:
# "The customer's issue was resolved, but it took
two steps more than necessary. Clearly optimize
steps for quicker resolution next time."
```

Clear evaluation feedback improves future agent performance.

Real-world Practical Example: Agent Decision-making Flow

Here's a practical, clear example illustrating all five building blocks clearly in a realistic scenario:

Building Block	Practical Scenario Example
Context	Customer has previously experienced login issues.
Perception	Clearly identify user's current login-related query.
Reasoning & Planning	Outline clear troubleshooting steps (password reset, verification).
Decision & Action	Clearly execute each troubleshooting step.
Feedback & Adaptation	Evaluate resolution clearly, adapt for efficiency next time.

Troubleshooting Common Decision-making Issues

Clear and practical troubleshooting advice for common decision-making issues:

Issue	Practical Troubleshooting Advice
Poor Contextual Responses	Provide clearer context data explicitly to the agent.
Inaccurate Perception	Clearly structure user input and refine input parsing.
Weak Reasoning or Planning	Clearly specify detailed steps explicitly in planning prompts.
Poor Decisions or Actions	Reinforce clearly structured plans to guide execution explicitly.

Best Practices for Effective Decision-making

Follow this practical best practices checklist clearly:

Explicitly provide clear and sufficient context.

Clearly structure input for accurate perception.

Develop reasoning clearly in explicit, structured steps.

Explicitly define criteria clearly for decisions.

Regularly evaluate and adapt based on feedback clearly.

Summary & Next Steps

In this practical, detailed section, you clearly learned the essential building blocks of effective autonomous agent decision-making:

Context

Perception

Reasoning and Planning

Decision and Action

Feedback and Adaptation

Clearly mastering these foundational elements ensures that your autonomous agents consistently make accurate, intelligent, and practical decisions.

Chapter 4: Building Simple Autonomous Agents

4.1 Planning Your Agent Project

Effective autonomous agent projects begin with clear, structured planning. Proper planning ensures your project runs smoothly, agents behave predictably, and outcomes align directly with real-world goals. This section guides you step-by-step through the practical process of clearly planning your first simple autonomous agent project.

Why Planning Matters

Clearly structured planning ensures your autonomous agent project will:

- **Align with clear, realistic goals.**
- **Simplify implementation steps.**
- **Prevent costly mistakes or rework.**
- **Improve agent performance and predictability.**
- **Accelerate overall project completion.**

Step-by-Step Guide to Planning Your Autonomous Agent Project

Follow this practical five-step process clearly to plan your project effectively:

Step	Planning Stage	Description
1	Define Clear Project Goals	Clearly articulate what you want your agent to achieve.
2	Identify Target Users and Context	Clearly understand who the agent serves and in what context.
3	Outline the Agent's Required Capabilities	Clearly specify features and functionalities required.
4	Choose Appropriate Tools and Models	Select the right language model and integrations clearly.

64

Step	Planning Stage	Description
5	Define Clear Success Criteria	Clearly define how you'll measure project success.

Let's practically explore each step clearly and thoroughly.

Step 1: Define Clear Project Goals

Clearly state exactly what you expect your autonomous agent to accomplish:

Good example goal statements:

- "Autonomously resolve common customer-support questions clearly and quickly."
- "Clearly generate concise, accurate financial summaries automatically from raw data."
- "Efficiently automate scheduling meetings and clearly communicating calendar updates."
- Clear, practical goals keep your project focused, manageable, and successful.

Step 2: Identify Target Users and Context

Clearly define who will use your agent, including their needs, roles, and context:

Aspect	Example (Customer Support Agent)
Target User	Customers seeking support
Context	Users experiencing common issues or queries

Typical Use Case Resolving password reset or billing inquiries clearly

Clear user context directly shapes how your agent is built and used practically.

Step 3: Outline the Agent's Required Capabilities

Clearly specify practical features and capabilities your agent must have:

Required Capability	Practical Example
Natural Language Understanding	Clearly interpret customer questions accurately
Access to Customer Data	Securely and clearly retrieve customer information
Issue Resolution	Clearly provide solutions step-by-step
Escalation	Clearly escalate unresolved issues automatically

Clear specification of these capabilities ensures efficient and effective agent development.

Step 4: Choose Appropriate Tools and Models

Clearly select the appropriate OpenAI model and external integrations practically:

Tool / Model	Reason for Practical Selection
Model (GPT-4 Turbo)	Cost-effective, efficient, suitable for common interactions clearly
Integration (REST APIs)	Practical integration with existing customer databases and support systems

Clear choices at this stage practically streamline implementation later.

Step 5: Define Clear Success Criteria

Clearly articulate how you will practically measure your project's success:

Success Criterion Example of Practical Measurement

Accuracy   Correctly resolving $\geq 90\%$ of queries

Efficiency   Response time ≤ 5 seconds per interaction

User Satisfaction Clear, positive customer feedback ratings $\geq 85\%$

Clear success criteria practically keep your project aligned with business value and user expectations.

Example: Planning a Customer Support Autonomous Agent (Case Study)

Here's a practical example demonstrating the clear planning process:

Project Name:

Autonomous Customer Support Agent

Planning Stage	Practical Planning Details Clearly Outlined
Project Goals	Quickly and clearly resolve common customer issues autonomously.
Target Users	Customers seeking immediate support solutions clearly.
Capabilities	Clearly interpret issues, access data, provide step-by-step solutions, escalate clearly if unresolved.
Tools/Models	GPT-4 Turbo (efficiency), REST API integrations with CRM.
Success Criteria	$\geq 90\%$ accuracy, ≤ 5 sec response, $\geq 85\%$ customer satisfaction.

This clearly structured planning process practically ensures project alignment, clarity, and effective execution.

Common Planning Mistakes & Troubleshooting

Practical advice clearly addressing common planning pitfalls:

Issue	Practical Troubleshooting Advice
Unclear Goals	Clearly articulate specific, measurable objectives explicitly.
Undefined User Context	Clearly specify detailed user needs and interaction context.
Missing Capabilities	Clearly document essential features and verify with stakeholders.
Poor Success Metrics	Clearly define specific, measurable, practical success criteria upfront.

Agent Project Planning Best Practices Checklist

Follow this practical checklist to ensure your plan is comprehensive and clear:

- Clearly defined, explicit project goals.
- Detailed understanding of target users and context.
- Explicitly documented agent capabilities.
- Appropriate selection of language models and tools.
- Clearly defined measurable success criteria.

Summary & Next Steps

In this practical section, you learned clearly and step-by-step how to plan your autonomous agent project effectively, including:

- Defining clear goals and success criteria explicitly.
- Understanding user contexts practically.
- Specifying necessary capabilities clearly.
- Selecting appropriate tools practically.

Clear, structured planning ensures smooth implementation, predictable agent behavior, and successful real-world outcomes.

4.2 Agent Creation Step-by-Step

Now that your autonomous agent project is clearly planned, it's time to practically build your first simple agent using OpenAI's SDK. This step-by-step tutorial guides you explicitly through creating an autonomous customer support agent, providing practical, tested code and clear explanations at every stage.

Project Goal:

Create a practical, autonomous customer support agent that can clearly and quickly respond to user questions related to billing and technical issues.

Step 1: Set Up Your Environment

Ensure you've clearly set up your project environment:

```bash
bash
```

```bash
mkdir autonomous-support-agent

cd autonomous-support-agent

python -m venv env

source env/bin/activate   # macOS/Linux

.\env\Scripts\activate   # Windows


pip install openai python-dotenv
```

Clearly configure your API key in a `.env` file:

```ini
ini
```

```
OPENAI_API_KEY="your-api-key-here"
```

Step 2: Agent Initialization and Configuration

Create a new file named `support_agent.py` and add clear initialization code:

```python
import openai

import os

from dotenv import load_dotenv


load_dotenv()
openai.api_key = os.getenv("OPENAI_API_KEY")


# Clearly define your agent prompt
system_prompt = """
You are an autonomous customer support agent.

Your primary task is to resolve user queries
clearly, politely, and concisely.

Escalate any unresolved issues clearly and
immediately.
"""
```

What's happening clearly here:

Securely loads your API key.

- Clearly defines the agent's behavior and role explicitly via the system prompt.

Step 3: Define a Practical Agent Function

Clearly implement a function to practically handle user questions:

python

```python
def autonomous_support_agent(user_query):
    response = openai.ChatCompletion.create(
        model="gpt-4-turbo",
        messages=[
            {"role": "system", "content":
system_prompt},
            {"role": "user", "content": user_query}
        ],
        temperature=0.3,  # Lower for concise,
accurate responses
        max_tokens=150
    )
    return
response.choices[0].message.content.strip()
```

Explanation clearly:

- Queries GPT-4 Turbo with clear system and user prompts.
- Adjusting `temperature` ensures accuracy and conciseness practically.

Step 4: Implement the Agent Interaction Loop

Clearly create an interactive loop to practically handle ongoing user questions:

python

```python
if __name__ == "__main__":
    print("Autonomous Customer Support Agent is
running. Type 'exit' to stop.\n")


    while True:
        user_input = input("User: ")


        if user_input.lower() == "exit":
            print("\nExiting Autonomous Customer
Support Agent. Goodbye!")
            break


        agent_response =
autonomous_support_agent(user_input)
        print(f"Agent: {agent_response}\n")
```

Practical outcome:

- Continuously accepts user input clearly.
- Provides immediate, clear responses.
- Exits cleanly when instructed practically.

Step 5: Run Your Autonomous Agent

Clearly execute your agent script practically from your terminal:

bash

```bash
python support_agent.py
```

Interact practically with your agent by asking clear questions like:

pgsql

```
User: How do I reset my billing password?


Agent: To reset your billing password, click
"Forgot Password" on the billing login page, enter
your registered email, and follow the instructions
sent to your email address.
```

Step 6: Practical Example of Complete Agent Interaction

Here's a practical interaction scenario illustrating clear and concise responses:

vbnet

```
User: I'm having trouble accessing my premium
subscription. What should I do?


Agent: Please verify you're logged in with the
email associated with your premium subscription. If
the issue persists, I recommend clearing your
browser cache and trying again. Let me know clearly
if the problem continues, and I'll escalate the
issue immediately.


User: I tried that, but it didn't work.


Agent: Thank you for confirming. I'll escalate this
issue clearly to our technical team immediately.
They will contact you shortly to resolve this
problem.
```

This practical example clearly demonstrates the agent's autonomous problem-solving capability and escalation logic.

Step 7: Troubleshooting Common Agent Creation Issues

Clear, practical advice for troubleshooting common issues:

Issue	Practical Troubleshooting Advice
Authentication Error	Clearly check `.env` file API key formatting.
Slow Agent Responses	Clearly reduce `max_tokens` or use GPT-4 Turbo for faster responses.
Poor Quality or Off-topic Answers	Clearly refine `system_prompt`, reduce `temperature`.

Step 8: Practical Tips for Enhancing Your Agent

Clearly consider practical enhancements:

- **Add memory management:** Retain context practically between interactions.
- **Integrate external APIs:** Fetch practical customer data clearly for more tailored responses.
- **Logging and Monitoring:** Clearly log interactions practically for performance tracking.

Best Practices Checklist for Creating Agents

- Clearly ensure your agent meets best practices practically:
- Clear, concise, and explicit system prompts.
- Optimal parameter tuning (`temperature`, `max_tokens`).
- Practical interaction loops for seamless user experiences.
- Clear escalation logic explicitly defined in prompts.
- Comprehensive testing of practical scenarios.

Summary & Next Steps

In this practical, step-by-step section, you clearly learned how to:

- Set up and configure your autonomous agent practically.
- Implement clear agent prompts and functions.
- Practically run and interact with your agent.
- Troubleshoot common practical issues.

You're now confidently equipped to build, test, and refine simple autonomous agents, preparing you clearly for advanced agent development.

4.3 Handling Tasks and Actions

Autonomous agents built using OpenAI's SDK perform tasks by clearly interpreting user instructions, breaking them down into actionable steps, and executing them reliably. Properly handling tasks and actions practically ensures your agent achieves accurate, predictable, and successful outcomes.

This section clearly explains how to practically structure and handle tasks and actions step-by-step, including tested, complete code examples.

Understanding Tasks and Actions

In autonomous agent workflows:

- **Tasks** are clear objectives the agent needs to accomplish (e.g., resolving a customer issue).
- **Actions** are individual steps or activities practically performed to complete a task (e.g., sending an email, querying a database).

Clear structuring of tasks and actions significantly improves agent reliability.

Step-by-Step Guide to Handling Tasks and Actions

Follow this clear, practical process:

Step	Task Handling Stage	Description
1	Clearly Define Tasks and Subtasks	Specify exactly what must be achieved.
2	Clearly Define Actions	Determine specific, actionable steps.
3	Practical Action Execution	Have the agent practically execute these actions.
4	Clear Action Monitoring and Logging	Track agent actions practically and clearly.
5	Practical Error Handling and Recovery	Gracefully handle unexpected issues clearly.

Let's practically explore each step with clear examples.

Step 1: Clearly Define Tasks and Subtasks

Explicitly outline tasks and subtasks practically for clear agent understanding:

Example Task: Customer Support Issue Resolution

Main task: Clearly resolve a user's billing issue.

Subtasks:

- Clearly identify user account information.
- Verify recent transactions clearly.
- Clearly identify discrepancies.
- Clearly provide resolution instructions or escalate if unresolved.
- Practical definition of tasks ensures clarity.

Step 2: Clearly Define Actions

Clearly specify the individual practical steps (actions) required to achieve tasks:

Subtask	Clearly Defined Actions
Identify account	Clearly query customer database via API
Verify transactions	Fetch recent billing transactions practically
Identify discrepancies	Practically analyze data clearly
Provide resolution	Clearly send concise instructions to user
Escalate issue	Clearly notify technical support via email

Clear action definition practically improves accuracy.

Step 3: Practical Action Execution

Practically implement autonomous action execution:

Complete practical code example:

python

```
import openai


# Clearly defined actions for customer support
def execute_action(action, context):
    if action == "identify_account":

        return f"Account identified:
{context['user_email']}"

    elif action == "verify_transactions":

        return "Transactions verified: No issues
found."

    elif action == "identify_discrepancies":

        return "Discrepancy found: Billing amount
mismatch."
```

```
    elif action == "provide_resolution":

        return "Resolution provided: Refund issued
clearly to user's account."

    elif action == "escalate_issue":

        return "Issue escalated clearly to
technical team."

    else:

        return "Unknown action clearly identified."


# Practical agent action loop

actions = ["identify_account",
"verify_transactions", "identify_discrepancies",
"provide_resolution"]


context = {"user_email": "customer@example.com"}


for action in actions:

    result = execute_action(action, context)

    print(f"Action: {action}, Result: {result}")
```

This practical example clearly demonstrates structured action execution.

Step 4: Clear Action Monitoring and Logging

Clearly monitor and log agent actions practically for transparency and troubleshooting:

```python
python


import logging
```

```python
# Set up clear practical logging
logging.basicConfig(filename='agent_actions.log',
level=logging.INFO, format='%(asctime)s
%(message)s')


def execute_and_log_action(action, context):
    result = execute_action(action, context)
    logging.info(f"Executed action: {action},
Result: {result}")
    return result


# Example usage practically
for action in actions:
    execute_and_log_action(action, context)
```

Practical logging clearly enhances monitoring and debugging.

Step 5: Practical Error Handling and Recovery

Implement clear, practical error handling for unexpected scenarios:

python

```python
def execute_action_safely(action, context):
    try:
        result = execute_action(action, context)
    except Exception as e:
        logging.error(f"Error executing action
'{action}': {str(e)}")
```

```python
        result = "Error clearly identified.
Escalating issue practically."

    return result


# Practically handle actions safely

for action in actions:

    response = execute_action_safely(action,
context)

    print(f"Safely executed action: {action},
Response: {response}")
```

Clear practical error handling ensures graceful recovery.

Practical Example: Complete Task and Action Flow

A full practical demonstration clearly showing structured task and action handling:

python

```python
# Full example practically structured

task_plan = {

    "Resolve Billing Issue": [

        "identify_account",

        "verify_transactions",

        "identify_discrepancies",

        "provide_resolution"

    ]

}
```

```python
for task, actions_list in task_plan.items():
    print(f"Starting task practically: {task}")
    for action in actions_list:
        response = execute_action_safely(action, context)
        print(f"Performed action: {action}, Result: {response}")
    print(f"Completed task clearly: {task}\n")
```

Practical and clear output example:

yaml

Starting task practically: Resolve Billing Issue

Performed action: identify_account, Result: Account identified: customer@example.com

Performed action: verify_transactions, Result: Transactions verified: No issues found.

Performed action: identify_discrepancies, Result: Discrepancy found: Billing amount mismatch.

Performed action: provide_resolution, Result: Resolution provided: Refund issued clearly to user's account.

Completed task clearly: Resolve Billing Issue

Troubleshooting Common Task and Action Issues

Clear, practical troubleshooting tips:

Issue	Practical Troubleshooting Advice
Undefined Action Errors	Clearly verify action names and definitions explicitly.

Issue	Practical Troubleshooting Advice
Failed External Integrations	Clearly check API connections, authentication, and endpoints.
Incorrect Task Handling	Explicitly refine your task and action planning clearly.

Best Practices Checklist

Follow clearly these best practices practically:

- Clearly define all tasks and subtasks explicitly.
- Define explicit, practical, actionable steps.
- Clearly implement structured execution loops.
- Practically monitor and log actions.
- Clearly implement robust error handling and recovery.

Summary & Next Steps

In this detailed, practical section, you clearly learned how to:

- Define tasks and actions explicitly and practically.
- Execute structured agent actions clearly and reliably.
- Monitor and practically log agent activities.
- Handle practical errors robustly and clearly.

You're now confidently prepared to build autonomous agents capable of practically executing clearly structured tasks and actions.

4.4 Practical Project: Autonomous Task Scheduler

In this practical project, you'll build a simple but powerful **Autonomous Task Scheduler Agent** using OpenAI's SDK. This agent autonomously manages, organizes, and schedules tasks based on user input, clearly demonstrating practical task handling, structured agent interactions, and integration with external tools.

Project

Goal:

Create an autonomous agent capable of:

- Understanding clearly defined tasks from user input.
- Automatically organizing tasks by priority.
- Suggesting clearly structured daily task schedules.

Real-world Relevance:

Such an agent is practically useful for managing personal productivity, automating workflows, and improving efficiency in both personal and professional settings.

Step-by-Step Guide

Follow these clear, practical steps to build your autonomous task scheduler:

Step	Stage	Description
1	Set Up Your Project Environment	Prepare your workspace practically.
2	Define Agent Initialization and Behavior	Clearly set agent prompts and context.
3	Create Task Management Functions	Practically handle and organize tasks.
4	Build the Scheduling Logic	Autonomously schedule tasks clearly.
5	Run and Test Your Autonomous Scheduler	Verify agent functionality practically.

Step 1: Set Up Your Project Environment

Create your project folder and activate a virtual environment:

```bash
bash
```

```
mkdir task-scheduler-agent

cd task-scheduler-agent

python -m venv env

source env/bin/activate      # macOS/Linux

.\env\Scripts\activate       # Windows


pip install openai python-dotenv
```

Clearly configure your API key in `.env`:

```ini
OPENAI_API_KEY="your-api-key-here"
```

Step 2: Define Agent Initialization and Behavior

Create a file `scheduler_agent.py` and add clearly defined prompts and setup:

```python
import openai
import os
from dotenv import load_dotenv


load_dotenv()
openai.api_key = os.getenv("OPENAI_API_KEY")


system_prompt = """
```

```
You are an autonomous task scheduler agent.

You clearly organize tasks by priority (high,
medium, low).

You then autonomously suggest a structured daily
schedule for these tasks.

"""
```

Step 3: Create Task Management Functions

Practically handle incoming tasks clearly and organize them by priority:

```python
python


def organize_tasks(tasks):

    prompt = f"""

    Organize the following tasks clearly by
priority (high, medium, low):


    {tasks}


    Provide your clear response in the format:

    High: [tasks]

    Medium: [tasks]

    Low: [tasks]
    """

    response = openai.ChatCompletion.create(
        model="gpt-4-turbo",
        messages=[{"role": "system", "content":
system_prompt},
```

```python
                {"role": "user", "content":
prompt}],
        temperature=0.2,
        max_tokens=300
    )
    return
response.choices[0].message.content.strip()
```

Step 4: Build the Scheduling Logic

Implement clear scheduling logic practically based on organized tasks:

python

```python
def generate_schedule(prioritized_tasks):
    prompt = f"""
    Given the prioritized tasks:
    {prioritized_tasks}


    Clearly create a practical daily schedule,
allocating appropriate times from 9 AM to 5 PM.
    Schedule high-priority tasks first, then
medium, then low.


    Format clearly as:
    [Time] - [Task]
    """

    response = openai.ChatCompletion.create(
        model="gpt-4-turbo",
```

```python
    messages=[{"role": "system", "content":
system_prompt},
                {"role": "user", "content":
prompt}],
        temperature=0.2,
        max_tokens=300
    )
    return
response.choices[0].message.content.strip()
```

Step 5: Run and Test Your Autonomous Scheduler

Implement practical interaction clearly in your main script:

python

```python
if __name__ == "__main__":
    print("Welcome to the Autonomous Task
Scheduler.\n")


    tasks = []
    print("Enter tasks clearly one by one (type
'done' to finish):")


    while True:
        task_input = input("Task: ")
        if task_input.lower() == "done":
            break
        tasks.append(task_input)
```

```
tasks_str = "\n".join(tasks)
prioritized_tasks = organize_tasks(tasks_str)


print("\nPrioritized Tasks:")
print(prioritized_tasks)


schedule = generate_schedule(prioritized_tasks)


print("\nAutonomous Daily Schedule:")
print(schedule)
```

Example Practical Interaction

Run your script:

bash

```
python scheduler_agent.py
```

Sample user input:

vbnet

```
Task: Finish project report
Task: Reply to emails
Task: Schedule team meeting
Task: Update software
Task: done
```

Practical output clearly:

```yaml
Prioritized Tasks:
High: Finish project report, Schedule team meeting
Medium: Update software
Low: Reply to emails


Autonomous Daily Schedule:
9:00 AM - 11:00 AM: Finish project report
11:00 AM - 12:00 PM: Schedule team meeting
12:00 PM - 1:00 PM: Lunch Break
1:00 PM - 2:30 PM: Update software
2:30 PM - 3:00 PM: Reply to emails
3:00 PM - 5:00 PM: Buffer time for additional tasks
or follow-ups
```

This clearly demonstrates autonomous scheduling capabilities practically.

Troubleshooting Common Issues

Clear, practical troubleshooting:

Issue	Practical Troubleshooting Advice
Poor Task Prioritization	Clearly refine prioritization prompt explicitly.
Unrealistic Scheduling	Clearly add explicit constraints on available times practically.

Issue	Practical Troubleshooting Advice
Long Response Times	Reduce `max_tokens` clearly or switch to a faster model practically.

Practical Enhancements

Consider clearly adding these enhancements practically:

- **Persistent task storage:** Practically save tasks to a database or file.
- **External calendar integration:** Practically integrate with calendar APIs (Google Calendar).
- **Interactive user interface:** Clearly implement a web or CLI-based UI practically.

Best Practices Checklist

Follow clearly:

- Explicitly defined agent role and clear prompts.
- Clear organization and prioritization of tasks.
- Practical and realistic scheduling logic.
- Robust error handling clearly implemented.
- Practical testing of realistic scenarios.

Summary & Next Steps

In this practical project, you:

- Clearly set up an autonomous task scheduler.
- Practically handled task input, prioritization, and scheduling.
- Verified functionality clearly through real-world examples.

You're now practically ready to advance to more complex agent capabilities, including advanced multi-agent systems and integrations.

Chapter 5: Advanced Agent Development Techniques

5.1 Complex Decision-making Logic

As your autonomous agent projects grow more sophisticated, clearly handling **complex decision-making logic** becomes crucial. Complex logic empowers your agents to practically reason through multi-step problems, manage conflicting priorities, and autonomously make nuanced decisions based on dynamic conditions.

This section provides practical, tested guidance to clearly implement advanced decision-making logic using OpenAI's SDK, complete with realistic examples and effective troubleshooting tips.

Understanding Complex Decision-making

Complex decision-making logic refers to an agent's practical ability to:

- Clearly analyze multiple variables simultaneously.
- Practically handle conditional logic (if/then scenarios).
- Clearly manage priorities and dependencies between tasks.
- Autonomously reason through multi-step processes.

These capabilities practically enable agents to tackle sophisticated real-world problems accurately.

Practical Approach to Complex Decision-making

Implement complex logic practically and clearly in five steps:

Step	Clearly Defined Stage	Practical Explanation
1	Define Decision-making Criteria Clearly	Clearly identify what factors impact decisions.
2	Model Conditional Logic	Clearly handle "if/then" and conditional scenarios.

Step	Clearly Defined Stage	Practical Explanation
3	Implement Structured Reasoning	Practically use explicit reasoning prompts.
4	Execute Autonomous Decisions	Practically run agent through logical reasoning.
5	Practical Monitoring and Validation	Clearly track and verify agent decisions.

Step 1: Define Decision-making Criteria Clearly

Explicitly define the criteria influencing agent decisions practically:

Real-world Example (Investment Advisor Agent):

- Risk tolerance level (high, medium, low)
- Investment amount available
- Current market conditions
- User investment goals (short-term vs. long-term)
- Clearly defined criteria practically improve decision quality.

Step 2: Model Conditional Logic Practically

Clearly implement conditional ("if/then") scenarios practically in prompts:

```python
decision_prompt = """
You are an autonomous investment advisor agent.

Clearly recommend an investment portfolio based on:
- Risk tolerance: medium
- Investment amount: $10,000
```

```
- Market condition: bearish


If market conditions are bearish, clearly
prioritize low-risk investments.

If investment amount is less than $50,000, clearly
suggest diversified, low-cost ETFs.


Provide your recommendation clearly and concisely.
"""
```

This explicit conditional logic practically guides nuanced decisions.

Step 3: Implement Structured Reasoning

Practically implement structured "chain-of-thought" reasoning clearly:

python

```
reasoning_prompt = """
You must clearly decide the best software update
strategy.


Consider:
1. Stability of the software.

2. Severity of reported bugs.

3. User impact.

4. Development team availability.


Clearly reason step-by-step:
- Evaluate each factor.
```

- Determine clearly if immediate update is necessary.

- Clearly state final recommendation.
"""

Structured reasoning practically ensures logical, transparent decisions.

Step 4: Execute Autonomous Decisions Practically

Use structured prompts clearly for decision execution practically:

python

```
import openai

response = openai.ChatCompletion.create(
    model="gpt-4o",
    messages=[
        {"role": "system", "content":
reasoning_prompt}
    ],
    temperature=0.3,
    max_tokens=250
)

decision_result =
response.choices[0].message.content.strip()
print(f"Agent's Decision:\n{decision_result}")
```

Clear execution practically yields reliable, structured decisions.

Step 5: Practical Monitoring and Validation

Implement clear logging and validation practically for transparency:

python

```
import logging


logging.basicConfig(filename='decision_logs.log',
level=logging.INFO, format='%(asctime)s
%(message)s')


def log_decision(decision):
    logging.info(f"Complex decision executed
clearly:\n{decision}")


log_decision(decision_result)
```

Clear logging practically simplifies monitoring and debugging.

Complete Practical Example: Autonomous Complex Decision-making

A practical, complete example clearly demonstrating end-to-end logic:

python

```
import openai
import logging
from dotenv import load_dotenv
import os


load_dotenv()
```

```python
openai.api_key = os.getenv("OPENAI_API_KEY")


logging.basicConfig(filename='complex_decision.log'
, level=logging.INFO, format='%(asctime)s
%(message)s')


prompt = """
You are an autonomous supply-chain management
agent.


Clearly decide the best strategy given:

- Low inventory of critical parts.

- Supplier delays.

- Upcoming product launch in 2 weeks.


Evaluate clearly and practically:

- Immediate sourcing from alternative suppliers.

- Cost vs. delay implications.

- Risks associated with delayed launch.


Clearly provide your step-by-step reasoning and
final decision.
"""


response = openai.ChatCompletion.create(
    model="gpt-4o",
```

```
    messages=[{"role": "system", "content":
prompt}],

    temperature=0.3,

    max_tokens=300

)


decision =
response.choices[0].message.content.strip()

print(f"Agent's Complex Decision:\n{decision}")


logging.info(f"Complex decision
executed:\n{decision}")
```

Clear Practical Output Example:

vbnet

```
Agent's Complex Decision:

Step-by-step reasoning:

1. Low inventory risks production delays.

2. Supplier delays further increase risks.

3. Alternative sourcing ensures parts availability
immediately.

4. Higher costs from alternatives outweigh risks of
delayed launch.


Final Decision:

Immediately source from alternative suppliers
clearly, despite higher short-term costs, to ensure
timely product launch.
```

Troubleshooting Common Complex Logic Issues

Clear, practical troubleshooting advice:

Issue	Practical Troubleshooting Advice
Poorly reasoned decisions	Clearly refine reasoning prompts explicitly.
Agent misunderstanding conditions	Explicitly and clearly structure conditional logic practically.
Ambiguous outcomes	Clearly instruct agent to provide explicit step-by-step reasoning.

Best Practices Checklist

- Clearly follow these best practices practically:
- Clearly defined, explicit decision-making criteria.
- Structured prompts clearly using conditional logic.
- Explicit step-by-step reasoning practically implemented.
- Clearly logged and monitored decisions practically.
- Robust error handling for unexpected decision outcomes.

Summary & Next Steps

In this practical, detailed section, you clearly learned how to implement:

- Explicitly defined decision-making criteria practically.
- Practical, structured reasoning clearly.
- Autonomous execution practically of complex decisions.
- Practical monitoring and validation clearly.

Clearly mastering these advanced techniques empowers your autonomous agents to handle increasingly sophisticated, real-world decision-making scenarios effectively.

5.2 Multi-Agent Collaboration and Coordination

As your autonomous agents grow more advanced, you'll find scenarios that practically benefit from multiple agents working together. **Multi-agent collaboration and coordination** involves clearly enabling agents to work autonomously, communicate effectively, and jointly accomplish complex goals.

This section provides clear, step-by-step guidance on practically implementing multi-agent systems using OpenAI's SDK, complete with realistic examples and practical troubleshooting tips.

Understanding Multi-Agent Systems

In practical multi-agent setups:

- Each agent autonomously specializes in distinct tasks or expertise.
- Agents clearly communicate, coordinate actions, and share information.
- Tasks are completed faster, more efficiently, and accurately.
- Practical examples include:
- Autonomous teams of customer support agents (billing, tech support, escalations).
- Autonomous research agents collaborating on complex data analysis.

Key Components of Multi-Agent Systems

Clear, practical multi-agent systems involve:

Component	Practical Role Clearly Defined
Specialized Agents	Clearly handle specific tasks or domains.
Communication Protocol	Clear, structured agent communication (JSON, structured prompts).
Coordination Logic	Clearly defines how agents collaborate autonomously.

Component	Practical Role Clearly Defined
Centralized Controller (optional)	Practically manages coordination explicitly.

Step-by-Step Guide to Multi-Agent Collaboration

Clearly implement multi-agent collaboration practically in five steps:

Step	Clearly Defined Stage	Practical Explanation
1	Define Clear Agent Roles	Explicitly specify individual agent responsibilities practically.
2	Establish Clear Communication Protocol	Clearly structure how agents interact and exchange information.
3	Implement Coordination Logic Clearly	Clearly define how decisions are made collectively practically.
4	Autonomous Agent Execution	Practically run agents in collaborative scenarios.
5	Practical Monitoring and Evaluation	Clearly verify and track agent collaboration practically.

Step 1: Define Clear Agent Roles

Clearly assign distinct roles explicitly to each agent practically:

Example (Customer Support Scenario):

- **Agent 1 (Billing Specialist):** Handles billing inquiries clearly.
- **Agent 2 (Technical Specialist):** Resolves technical issues practically.
- **Agent 3 (Escalation Agent):** Clearly handles unresolved or complex issues practically.

Explicit role definition clearly enhances collaboration.

Step 2: Establish Clear Communication Protocol

Clearly define structured communication practically (using JSON or structured messages):

Clear JSON Example:

```json
{
  "sender": "Billing Specialist",
  "receiver": "Technical Specialist",
  "message": "Customer reports billing access issue; may involve technical login problem.",
  "urgency": "high",
  "request_action": "investigate login system"
}
```

Clear structured messages practically ensure reliable interactions.

Step 3: Implement Coordination Logic Clearly

Explicitly define clear coordination logic practically:

- Clearly define how agents decide tasks or escalate issues.
- Explicitly specify decision-making procedures.

Example Logic (pseudo-code):

```python
def coordinate(agent_messages):
    if agent_messages["urgency"] == "high":
        assign_task(agent_messages["receiver"])
```

```python
    elif agent_messages["receiver"] == "Escalation
Agent":

        escalate_immediately()
```

Clear logic ensures predictable, coordinated behavior practically.

Step 4: Autonomous Agent Execution

Practically demonstrate clear multi-agent interaction explicitly:

python

```python
import openai


def communicate(sender, receiver, message):
    prompt = f"""
    You are {receiver}. Clearly respond to the
following message from {sender}:
    '{message}'
    """
    response = openai.ChatCompletion.create(
        model="gpt-4-turbo",
        messages=[{"role": "system", "content":
prompt}],
        temperature=0.2,
        max_tokens=150
    )
    return
response.choices[0].message.content.strip()
```

```python
# Practical interaction clearly

billing_issue = "Customer cannot access billing
portal."


# Billing Specialist clearly initiates
communication

tech_response = communicate("Billing Specialist",
"Technical Specialist", billing_issue)

print(f"Technical Specialist Response:
{tech_response}")
```

Step 5: Practical Monitoring and Evaluation

Clearly log and monitor multi-agent interactions practically:

python

```python
import logging


logging.basicConfig(filename='multi_agent_logs.log'
, level=logging.INFO, format='%(asctime)s
%(message)s')


def log_communication(sender, receiver, message,
response):

    logging.info(f"{sender} clearly messaged
{receiver}: '{message}'")

    logging.info(f"{receiver}'s clear response:
'{response}'")
```

```python
log_communication("Billing Specialist", "Technical
Specialist", billing_issue, tech_response)
```

Clear logs practically enhance debugging and transparency.

Complete Practical Multi-Agent Example

Full example demonstrating clear multi-agent collaboration practically:

python

```python
import openai
import logging
from dotenv import load_dotenv
import os


load_dotenv()
openai.api_key = os.getenv("OPENAI_API_KEY")


logging.basicConfig(filename='multi_agent_system.lo
g', level=logging.INFO, format='%(asctime)s
%(message)s')


def agent_interaction(sender, receiver, task):
    prompt = f"""
    You are {receiver}. Clearly handle this task
from {sender}:
    '{task}'
    """

    response = openai.ChatCompletion.create(
```

```python
        model="gpt-4-turbo",

        messages=[{"role": "system", "content":
prompt}],

        temperature=0.2,

        max_tokens=150

    )

    return
response.choices[0].message.content.strip()


# Practical scenario clearly

billing_task = "Customer unable to pay invoice cue
to website error."


tech_response = agent_interaction("Billing
Specialist", "Technical Specialist", billing_task)

log_communication("Billing Specialist", "Technical
Specialist", billing_task, tech_response)


if "escalate" in tech_response.lower():

    escalation_response =
agent_interaction("Technical Specialist",
"Escalation Agent", tech_response)

    log_communication("Technical Specialist",
"Escalation Agent", tech_response,
escalation_response)


    print(f"Escalation Agent Response:
{escalation_response}")

else:
```

```
print(f"Technical Specialist Response:
{tech_response}")
```

Troubleshooting Common Multi-Agent Issues

Clear, practical troubleshooting advice explicitly:

Issue	Practical Troubleshooting Advice
Poor Agent Communication	Clearly structure messages explicitly (JSON recommended).
Coordination Failures	Explicitly refine coordination logic practically.
Agent Overlap or Conflict	Clearly define roles and responsibilities practically.

Best Practices Checklist

Clearly follow these practical guidelines explicitly:

- Clearly defined and explicitly assigned agent roles.
- Clear, structured communication protocols practically implemented.
- Explicit coordination logic practically defined.
- Practically monitored multi-agent interactions clearly.
- Clear and robust error handling implemented practically.

Summary & Next Steps

In this practical, detailed section, you clearly learned how to:

- Practically define clear agent roles explicitly.
- Clearly implement structured communication protocols.
- Practically coordinate multiple autonomous agents explicitly.
- Clearly monitor and practically evaluate interactions.

Clearly mastering these advanced multi-agent techniques empowers you to build sophisticated autonomous systems capable of practically tackling complex, real-world tasks collaboratively.

5.3 Managing Agent Memory and Context

Effectively managing **agent memory and context** practically enables your autonomous agents to maintain coherent, personalized, and intelligent interactions over multiple sessions. Clear memory management ensures agents remember past interactions, learn user preferences, and deliver consistent, context-aware responses.

In this section, you'll practically learn clear, step-by-step approaches for implementing effective memory management techniques using OpenAI's SDK, along with practical code examples and troubleshooting advice.

Why Agent Memory and Context Matters

Clear memory management practically helps agents to:

- Remember and clearly reference previous conversations or decisions.
- Provide consistent, personalized user experiences practically.
- Handle complex multi-step tasks with reliable continuity clearly.

Types of Agent Memory

Practically, agent memory includes:

Memory Type	Practical Use Cases Clearly Defined
Short-Term Memory	Remembering recent interactions clearly within one session.
Long-Term Memory	Persisting information practically across multiple sessions.

Both clearly play essential roles in enhancing autonomous agents practically.

Step-by-Step Guide to Managing Memory and Context

Implement memory management practically and clearly in five steps:

Step	Clearly Defined Stage	Practical Explanation
1	Define Clear Memory Structure	Clearly specify how memory is stored explicitly.
2	Capture Context Practically	Clearly record important user interactions practically.
3	Retrieve and Use Context Clearly	Explicitly use stored memory in future interactions practically.
4	Persist Memory Practically	Clearly store and manage long-term memory practically.
5	Manage and Clear Memory Explicitly	Practically manage memory to maintain efficiency clearly.

Step 1: Define Clear Memory Structure

Clearly implement memory practically using structured formats (lists, dictionaries):

Simple Example (Python Dictionary):

```python

agent_memory = {
    "user_history": [],
    "preferences": {},
    "recent_actions": []
}
```

Clear structures practically simplify memory handling explicitly.

Step 2: Capture Context Practically

Practically capture and store interactions clearly:

```python

def capture_interaction(user_message,
agent_response):

    agent_memory["user_history"].append({

        "user": user_message,

        "agent": agent_response

    })
```

Practically capturing context ensures accuracy explicitly.

Step 3: Retrieve and Use Context Clearly

Clearly reference memory in interactions practically:

```python

def get_recent_context():

    history = agent_memory["user_history"][-5:]  #
Clearly retrieves last 5 interactions practically

    context_summary = "\n".join([f"User:
{h['user']}\nAgent: {h['agent']}" for h in
history])

    return context_summary
```

Clear retrieval practically enhances relevance explicitly.

Step 4: Persist Memory Practically

Clearly store memory practically using JSON files:

python

```python
import json

def save_memory():
    with open("agent_memory.json", "w") as file:
        json.dump(agent_memory, file, indent=4)


def load_memory():
    global agent_memory
    try:
        with open("agent_memory.json", "r") as file:
            agent_memory = json.load(file)
    except FileNotFoundError:
        agent_memory = {"user_history": [], "preferences": {}, "recent_actions": []}
```

Practical persistence ensures memory availability across sessions clearly.

Step 5: Manage and Clear Memory Explicitly

Practically clear or limit memory clearly:

python

```python
def clear_old_memory(limit=50):
    if len(agent_memory["user_history"]) > limit:
        agent_memory["user_history"] = agent_memory["user_history"][-limit:]
```

Clearly managing memory practically prevents memory overload explicitly.

Complete Practical Example: Memory-Enhanced Agent

Full practical example explicitly demonstrating memory management clearly:

python

```python
import openai
import json
from dotenv import load_dotenv
import os


load_dotenv()
openai.api_key = os.getenv("OPENAI_API_KEY")


memory_file = "agent_memory.json"


def load_memory():
    try:
        with open(memory_file, "r") as file:
            return json.load(file)
    except FileNotFoundError:
        return {"user_history": []}


def save_memory(memory):
    with open(memory_file, "w") as file:
        json.dump(memory, file, indent=4)
```

```python
agent_memory = load_memory()


def agent_response(user_message):
    recent_context = "\n".join([f"User:
{h['user']}\nAgent: {h['agent']}" for h in
agent_memory["user_history"][-3:]])


    prompt = f"""
    You are an autonomous customer support agent.
    Consider recent context:
    {recent_context}

    Clearly respond to user's current query:
    '{user_message}'
    """


    response = openai.ChatCompletion.create(
        model="gpt-4-turbo",
        messages=[{"role": "system", "content":
prompt}],
        temperature=0.3,
        max_tokens=200
    ).choices[0].message.content.strip()


    # Practically capture new interaction clearly
    agent_memory["user_history"].append({"user":
user_message, "agent": response})
```

```python
    save_memory(agent_memory)

    return response


# Practical interaction clearly
if __name__ == "__main__":
    while True:
        user_input = input("User: ")
        if user_input.lower() == "exit":
            break
        print("Agent:", agent_response(user_input))
```

Troubleshooting Common Memory Issues

Clear, practical troubleshooting explicitly:

Issue	Practical Troubleshooting Advice
Memory Overload	Clearly implement explicit memory clearing practically.
Incorrect Context Retrieval	Explicitly verify memory retrieval logic clearly.
Persistent Storage Issues	Practically check JSON file paths and permissions clearly.

Best Practices Checklist

Clearly follow practical guidelines explicitly:

- Clearly structured explicit memory definition practically.
- Practical, explicit context capturing methods.
- Clear retrieval and referencing of memory practically.

- Practically persistent memory storage explicitly defined.
- Explicit memory management and clearing practically.

Summary & Next Steps

In this practical, detailed section, you explicitly learned how to:

- Clearly structure and manage memory practically.
- Capture, store, and retrieve context explicitly.
- Practically persist and manage memory over time clearly.
- Clearly mastering memory management practically enables your agents to deliver personalized, coherent, and effective long-term interactions.

You're now confidently ready for even more advanced capabilities, including external integrations and real-world deployments.

5.4 Advanced Prompt Engineering (Chain-of-Thought, Few-Shot)

To build truly effective autonomous agents, mastering **advanced prompt engineering techniques** practically is crucial. Techniques such as **Chain-of-Thought (CoT)** and **Few-Shot Prompting** clearly enable your agents to reason logically, tackle complex problems effectively, and produce accurate, reliable results consistently.

In this section, you'll practically learn clear, step-by-step guidance on explicitly using advanced prompt engineering methods with OpenAI's SDK, complete with tested, practical code examples and troubleshooting tips.

Understanding Advanced Prompt Engineering

Two highly practical techniques clearly enhance agent performance:

- **Chain-of-Thought (CoT):** Agents clearly break down complex problems explicitly into logical steps.
- **Few-Shot Prompting:** Agents clearly learn from explicitly provided examples practically to guide responses.

Using these techniques practically improves clarity, reasoning accuracy, and consistency explicitly.

Chain-of-Thought (CoT) Prompting

CoT explicitly guides the agent to reason practically step-by-step clearly through complex tasks.

Example of Standard Prompt (without CoT):

```pgsql
What is the total cost of 3 books, each priced at
$15, and a shipping fee of $5?
```

Example of CoT Prompt:

```pgsql
What is the total cost of 3 books, each priced at
$15, and a shipping fee of $5?

Clearly explain your answer step-by-step.
```

Practical Example Implementation:

```python
import openai

prompt_cot = """
You are an autonomous shopping assistant agent.

Calculate the total cost of the following clearly,
step-by-step:
```

- 4 shirts at $20 each

- 2 pairs of shoes at $50 each

- Shipping fee: $10

Provide your reasoning explicitly and clearly.

"""


```python
response = openai.ChatCompletion.create(
    model="gpt-4-turbo",
    messages=[{"role": "system", "content":
prompt_cot}],
    temperature=0.2,
    max_tokens=200
)


print("Chain-of-Thought Response:\n",
response.choices[0].message.content.strip())
```

Clear Practical Output:

```bash

Chain-of-Thought Response:
Step-by-step calculation:
1. Shirts: 4 x $20 = $80
2. Shoes: 2 x $50 = $100
3. Shipping: $10
Total: $80 + $100 + $10 = $190
```

Few-Shot Prompting

Clearly providing explicit examples practically helps the agent learn expected response patterns.

Example Few-Shot Prompt Clearly:

python

```
few_shot_prompt = """
You are an autonomous customer support agent.


Example:

Customer: I can't log into my account.

Agent: Please try resetting your password by
clicking "Forgot Password" on the login page.


Customer: How do I update my billing info?

Agent: You can update billing details by going to
your account settings and selecting "Billing
Information."


Now respond clearly:

Customer: How do I cancel my subscription?

Agent:
"""
```

Practical Implementation Clearly:

python

```python
response = openai.ChatCompletion.create(
    model="gpt-4-turbo",
    messages=[{"role": "system", "content":
few_shot_prompt}],
    temperature=0.2,
    max_tokens=100
)


print("Few-Shot Response:\n",
response.choices[0].message.content.strip())
```

Clear Practical Output:

```vbnet
Few-Shot Response:
You can cancel your subscription by going to your
account settings, selecting "Subscriptions," and
clicking "Cancel Subscription."
```

Combining Chain-of-Thought and Few-Shot Practically

Practically combining both techniques explicitly enhances reasoning further:

```python
combined_prompt = """
You are an autonomous math assistant.


Example:
```

Problem: If one apple costs $2, what is the cost of 5 apples?

Solution step-by-step:

1. Cost per apple: $2

2. Total cost for 5 apples: 5 x $2 = $10

Final Answer: $10

Now solve clearly step-by-step:

Problem: A box contains 6 pencils priced at $3 each and 2 notebooks priced at $5 each. What is the total cost?

Solution step-by-step:

"""


```
response = openai.ChatCompletion.create(

    model="gpt-4-turbo",

    messages=[{"role": "system", "content":
combined_prompt}],

    temperature=0.2,

    max_tokens=200

)


print("Combined CoT and Few-Shot Response:\n",
response.choices[0].message.content.strip())
```

Clear Practical Output:

nginx

```
Combined CoT and Few-Shot Response:
1. Pencils: 6 x $3 = $18
2. Notebooks: 2 x $5 = $10
3. Total cost: $18 + $10 = $28
Final Answer: $28
```

Practical Troubleshooting Tips

Clear, explicit troubleshooting for advanced prompts practically:

Issue	Practical Troubleshooting Advice
Incomplete Reasoning	Explicitly instruct agent clearly to provide step-by-step explanations.
Incorrect Examples in Few-Shot	Clearly provide accurate and relevant few-shot examples explicitly.
Excessively Verbose Responses	Practically limit `max_tokens`, and explicitly ask for concise responses.

Best Practices Checklist

Clearly follow practical guidelines explicitly:

- Clearly instruct explicit step-by-step reasoning (CoT).
- Provide clearly structured explicit examples practically (Few-Shot).
- Combine techniques practically for complex reasoning explicitly.
- Practically test and refine prompt clarity explicitly.
- Clearly handle errors and troubleshoot explicitly.

Summary & Next Steps

In this practical, detailed section, you explicitly learned:

- How to practically implement Chain-of-Thought clearly for logical reasoning.
- Clearly using Few-Shot examples explicitly to guide agent responses practically.
- Practically combining advanced prompt techniques explicitly.
- Mastering these advanced prompt engineering techniques practically enables your agents to handle complex, real-world problems accurately, clearly, and effectively.

You're now confidently ready for further advanced agent capabilities, including integration with external systems and sophisticated workflows.

5.5 Project: Context-Aware Customer Support Agent

In this advanced practical project, you'll build a fully functional **Context-Aware Customer Support Agent** using OpenAI's SDK. This agent practically leverages memory and advanced prompt techniques (Chain-of-Thought, Few-Shot) to clearly deliver personalized, context-aware interactions, autonomously resolving customer queries with high accuracy.

Project

Goal:

Create an autonomous customer support agent capable of:

- Remembering clearly past interactions (context).
- Providing personalized, coherent responses explicitly.
- Practically using advanced prompt engineering (CoT, Few-Shot).

Real-world Relevance:

Practical applications include automated customer support, improving user satisfaction through personalized interactions, and reducing support costs clearly and practically.

Step-by-Step Guide

Follow these clear, practical steps explicitly to build your context-aware agent:

Step	Clearly Defined Stage	Practical Explanation
1	Set Up Environment Practically	Clearly prepare your workspace explicitly.
2	Implement Context-Aware Memory Clearly	Practically handle customer interactions explicitly.
3	Advanced Prompt Engineering Practically	Implement CoT and Few-Shot explicitly.
4	Autonomous Agent Interaction Clearly	Run practical context-aware interactions explicitly.
5	Practical Testing and Monitoring	Clearly verify agent functionality practically.

Step 1: Set Up Environment Practically

Create your workspace explicitly:

bash

```
mkdir context-support-agent
cd context-support-agent
python -m venv env
source env/bin/activate    # macOS/Linux
.\env\Scripts\activate     # Windows

pip install openai python-dotenv
```

Configure your API key clearly in .env:

```ini
OPENAI_API_KEY="your-api-key-here"
```

Step 2: Implement Context-Aware Memory Clearly

Practically manage and store context clearly (`agent_memory.json`):

```python
import json

memory_file = "agent_memory.json"

def load_memory():
    try:
        with open(memory_file, "r") as file:
            return json.load(file)
    except FileNotFoundError:
        return {"user_history": []}

def save_memory(memory):
    with open(memory_file, "w") as file:
        json.dump(memory, file, indent=4)

agent_memory = load_memory()

def update_memory(user_message, agent_response):
```

```python
agent_memory["user_history"].append({
    "user": user_message,
    "agent": agent_response
})
save_memory(agent_memory)
```

Step 3: Advanced Prompt Engineering Practically

Implement CoT and Few-Shot clearly:

python

```python
import openai
import os
from dotenv import load_dotenv

load_dotenv()
openai.api_key = os.getenv("OPENAI_API_KEY")

def generate_agent_response(user_message,
recent_context):
    prompt = f"""
    You are a context-aware customer support agent.

    Recent interactions explicitly:
    {recent_context}

    Examples explicitly:
```

Customer: How do I reset my password?

Agent: Clearly click "Forgot Password" on the login page and follow the instructions.

Customer: My invoice has errors.

Agent: Let me verify your invoice details and assist you clearly.

Now respond clearly and step-by-step to:

Customer: {user_message}

"""

```python
response = openai.ChatCompletion.create(
    model="gpt-4-turbo",
    messages=[{"role": "system", "content": prompt}],
    temperature=0.3,
    max_tokens=200
)


    return response.choices[0].message.content.strip()
```

Step 4: Autonomous Agent Interaction Clearly

Implement practical interaction explicitly (main.py):

python

```python
def get_recent_context():
    recent_interactions =
agent_memory["user_history"][-3:]  # Last 3
interactions practically

    context_summary = "\n".join([f"Customer:
{h['user']}\nAgent: {h['agent']}" for h in
recent_interactions])

    return context_summary


if __name__ == "__main__":
    print("Context-Aware Customer Support Agent
(type 'exit' to quit)")


    while True:
        user_message = input("Customer: ")
        if user_message.lower() == "exit":
            break


        recent_context = get_recent_context()
        agent_response =
generate_agent_response(user_message,
recent_context)


        print("Agent:", agent_response)
        update_memory(user_message, agent_response)
```

Step 5: Practical Testing and Monitoring

Clearly test practical interaction explicitly by running:

```bash

python main.py
```
Practical Example Interaction Explicitly:

```vbnet

Customer: How do I update my billing information?

Agent: You can clearly update billing information
by going to your account settings and selecting
"Billing Details."


Customer: I did that, but I'm still getting charged
incorrectly.

Agent: Let me explicitly verify your billing
details and recent transactions to identify
discrepancies clearly.


Customer: Can you also check my previous invoices?

Agent: Absolutely. I'll clearly review your
previous invoices for any billing discrepancies
explicitly and update you shortly.
```

Practical Troubleshooting Tips

Clear, practical advice explicitly:

Issue	Practical Troubleshooting Advice
Poor Memory Context	Clearly verify memory loading/saving explicitly.
Weak Reasoning or Responses	Explicitly refine your CoT and Few-Shot prompts clearly.

Issue	Practical Troubleshooting Advice
Slow Responses	Clearly limit `max_tokens` and reduce prompt complexity practically.

Practical Enhancements

Clearly consider these explicit enhancements practically:

- **Integration with CRM:** Practically integrate customer data explicitly.
- **Persistent long-term memory:** Clearly store interactions explicitly in databases practically.
- **Error handling and escalation logic:** Explicitly implement escalation clearly for unresolved issues.

Best Practices Checklist

Clearly follow practical guidelines explicitly:

- Clearly structured explicit memory practically implemented.
- Practical advanced prompt engineering explicitly used.
- Explicitly context-aware responses practically verified.
- Practical logging and monitoring explicitly implemented.
- Robust error handling clearly included practically.

Summary & Next Steps

In this practical, detailed section, you explicitly learned:

- How to practically manage clear context and memory explicitly.
- Practically using advanced prompt engineering explicitly.
- Implementing clear autonomous context-aware interactions practically.

You've practically built a sophisticated, personalized customer support agent clearly capable of delivering effective, consistent support autonomously.

5.4 Advanced Prompt Engineering

Effective **prompt engineering** significantly enhances your autonomous agents' reasoning and problem-solving capabilities. By clearly implementing advanced techniques like **Chain-of-Thought (CoT)** and **Few-Shot prompting**, you enable agents to practically handle complex scenarios, reason step-by-step, and consistently produce accurate and reliable responses.

This section practically explains these techniques clearly, with step-by-step examples and explicit guidance.

Understanding Advanced Prompt Techniques

Two critical prompt techniques practically used for autonomous agents:

- **Chain-of-Thought (CoT):** Clearly guides agents through explicit step-by-step reasoning.
- **Few-Shot Prompting:** Clearly provides practical examples explicitly, guiding agents toward accurate responses.

Together, these methods practically improve accuracy, clarity, and consistency explicitly.

Chain-of-Thought (CoT) Prompting

Chain-of-Thought explicitly encourages agents to clearly reason through problems step-by-step, enhancing accuracy, especially in complex scenarios.

Example of a standard prompt (without CoT):

```swift
```

```
Calculate the total price of 5 pens costing $2 each
and 3 notebooks costing $4 each.
```

Clear CoT Prompt Example:

```pgsql
```

129

Calculate the total price of 5 pens costing $2 each and 3 notebooks costing $4 each.

Explain your solution clearly, step-by-step.

Practical Implementation Example:

python

```python
import openai

cot_prompt = """
You are an autonomous assistant.

Solve this clearly, step-by-step:
- 5 pens at $2 each
- 3 notebooks at $4 each

Provide your explicit reasoning clearly.
"""

response = openai.ChatCompletion.create(
    model="gpt-4-turbo",
    messages=[{"role": "system", "content": cot_prompt}],
    temperature=0.2,
    max_tokens=200
)
```

```python
print("Chain-of-Thought Response:\n",
response.choices[0].message.content.strip())
```

Clear Practical Output:

```bash
Chain-of-Thought Response:

Step-by-step solution:

1. Pens: 5 pens × $2 = $10

2. Notebooks: 3 notebooks × $4 = $12

3. Total price: $10 + $12 = $22

Final Answer: $22
```

Few-Shot Prompting

Few-Shot prompting practically involves clearly providing explicit examples that demonstrate the expected response style or content.

Example Few-Shot Prompt:

```python
few_shot_prompt = """
You are a customer support agent.


Example 1:

Customer: How do I reset my password?

Agent: You can reset your password by clicking
"Forgot Password" on the login page and following
the instructions.
```

Example 2:

Customer: Where can I update my payment method?

Agent: To update your payment method, go to your account settings and click "Billing".

Now respond clearly:

Customer: How do I cancel my subscription?

Agent:

"""

Practical Implementation Example:

python

```python
response = openai.ChatCompletion.create(
    model="gpt-4-turbo",
    messages=[{"role": "system", "content":
few_shot_prompt}],
    temperature=0.2,
    max_tokens=100
)


print("Few-Shot Response:\n",
response.choices[0].message.content.strip())
```

Clear Practical Output:

vbnet

Few-Shot Response:

You can cancel your subscription by going to your account settings, selecting "Subscription," and clicking "Cancel Subscription."

Combining Chain-of-Thought and Few-Shot Prompting

Practically combining CoT and Few-Shot methods explicitly delivers highly effective results:

Clear Combined Prompt Example:

python

```
combined_prompt = """
You are an autonomous math assistant.


Example:
Problem: If 4 apples cost $12, what is the cost of
7 apples?

Step-by-step solution:

1. Cost per apple: $12 ÷ 4 = $3

2. Total for 7 apples: 7 × $3 = $21

Final Answer: $21


Now solve step-by-step clearly:

Problem: A store sells pencils at $1 each and
erasers at $2 each. How much will 3 pencils and 5
erasers cost?

Step-by-step solution:
"""
```

```python
response = openai.ChatCompletion.create(
    model="gpt-4-turbo",
    messages=[{"role": "system", "content":
combined_prompt}],
    temperature=0.2,
    max_tokens=200
)


print("Combined CoT and Few-Shot Response:\n",
response.choices[0].message.content.strip())
```

Clear Practical Output:

```
nginx


Combined CoT and Few-Shot Response:
1. Pencils: 3 × $1 = $3
2. Erasers: 5 × $2 = $10
3. Total cost: $3 + $10 = $13
Final Answer: $13
```

Practical Troubleshooting Advice

Clear, explicit troubleshooting practically:

Issue	Practical Troubleshooting Advice
Incomplete Reasoning	Explicitly instruct clear step-by-step reasoning practically.
Incorrect Example Usage	Clearly verify examples provided explicitly.

Issue	Practical Troubleshooting Advice
Excessively Long Responses	Practically limit `max_tokens` and explicitly request concise answers.

Advanced Prompt Best Practices Checklist

Clearly follow these explicit guidelines practically:

- Explicitly instruct clear step-by-step reasoning (CoT).
- Clearly provide explicit practical examples (Few-Shot).
- Combine CoT and Few-Shot explicitly for complex scenarios practically.
- Practically test and refine prompts clearly.
- Explicit error handling practically implemented.

Complete Practical Example: Advanced Prompting

Full, practical example clearly demonstrating explicit advanced prompting:

python

```
import openai
import os
from dotenv import load_dotenv


load_dotenv()
openai.api_key = os.getenv("OPENAI_API_KEY")


advanced_prompt = """
You are an autonomous troubleshooting assistant.
```

Example:

Issue: Laptop won't turn on.

Step-by-step solution:

1. Verify the laptop charger connection.

2. Check if the battery indicator shows charging.

3. Attempt a hard reset (hold power button for 15 seconds).

4. If issue persists, recommend contacting technical support.

Final Advice: Follow these steps clearly.

Now solve step-by-step explicitly:

Issue: Printer isn't printing, though connected and showing online.

Step-by-step solution:
"""

```python
response = openai.ChatCompletion.create(
    model="gpt-4-turbo",
    messages=[{"role": "system", "content":
advanced_prompt}],
    temperature=0.3,
    max_tokens=250
)


print("Advanced Prompting Response:\n",
response.choices[0].message.content.strip())
```

Clear Practical Output:

```
arduino


Advanced Prompting Response:

1. Check printer for error messages or blinking
lights clearly.

2. Verify ink or toner levels explicitly.

3. Restart printer clearly and attempt a test
print.

4. Check print queue clearly and clear pending
print jobs explicitly.

5. Reinstall printer drivers if necessary.

Final Advice: Clearly follow these steps; if the
printer still doesn't print, contact technical
support.
```

Summary & Next Steps

In this practical, detailed section, you've explicitly learned:

- Clearly implementing Chain-of-Thought prompting explicitly.
- Practical use of Few-Shot examples explicitly.
- Practically combining advanced prompt techniques clearly.

Mastering these practical advanced prompt techniques explicitly ensures your autonomous agents consistently deliver accurate, coherent, and effective responses clearly.

5.5 Project: Context-Aware Customer Support Agent

In this practical, hands-on project, you'll build an intelligent, **Context-Aware Customer Support Agent** using OpenAI's SDK. This autonomous agent will leverage advanced memory techniques, context retention, and sophisticated prompt engineering methods to deliver personalized, accurate, and efficient customer support.

Project

Goal:

Develop an autonomous agent capable of:

- Retaining clear context and memory across multiple user interactions.
- Using advanced prompting techniques (Chain-of-Thought and Few-Shot) to improve reasoning and responses.
- Providing personalized, context-aware customer support.

Real-World Relevance:

This practical agent can autonomously handle customer queries, significantly improving customer satisfaction, reducing workload, and streamlining customer service operations.

Step-by-Step Implementation

Follow these practical steps clearly:

Step	Clearly Defined Stage	Practical Explanation
1	Set Up Project Environment Practically	Prepare environment explicitly.
2	Context and Memory Management Clearly	Implement clear context retention practically.
3	Advanced Prompt Engineering Explicitly	Incorporate CoT and Few-Shot prompts clearly.
4	Autonomous Interaction Practically	Enable clear context-aware interactions explicitly.
5	Testing, Logging, and Troubleshooting	Verify and monitor practically.

Step 1: Set Up Project Environment Practically

Clearly set up your environment explicitly:

bash

```
mkdir context-support-agent
cd context-support-agent
python -m venv env
source env/bin/activate    # macOS/Linux
.\env\Scripts\activate     # Windows

pip install openai python-dotenv
```

Configure your API key in .env:

ini

```
OPENAI_API_KEY="your-api-key-here"
```

Step 2: Context and Memory Management Clearly

Implement explicit context management practically (memory.py):

python

```
import json

memory_file = "agent_memory.json"

def load_memory():
```

```python
    try:
        with open(memory_file, "r") as file:
            return json.load(file)
    except FileNotFoundError:
        return {"interactions": []}


def save_memory(memory):
    with open(memory_file, "w") as file:
        json.dump(memory, file, indent=4)


memory = load_memory()


def update_memory(user_msg, agent_response):
    memory["interactions"].append({"user":
user_msg, "agent": agent_response})
    save_memory(memory)


def get_recent_context(n=3):
    recent = memory["interactions"][-n:]
    context = "\n".join([f"Customer:
{i['user']}\nAgent: {i['agent']}" for i in recent])
    return context
```

Step 3: Advanced Prompt Engineering Explicitly

Implement Chain-of-Thought and Few-Shot prompts practically
(agent.py):

python

```python
import openai

import os

from dotenv import load_dotenv

from memory import update_memory,
get_recent_context


load_dotenv()

openai.api_key = os.getenv("OPENAI_API_KEY")


def generate_response(user_input):

    recent_context = get_recent_context()

    prompt = f"""

    You are a context-aware customer support agent.


    Recent interactions explicitly:

    {recent_context}


    Examples clearly:

    Customer: How do I change my password?

    Agent: Go to your account settings and click
"Change Password." Follow the instructions
explicitly.


    Customer: I have billing errors on my invoice.

    Agent: Let me check your invoice details and
assist you clearly.
```

```
    Now clearly respond step-by-step explicitly to:
    Customer: {user_input}
    """


    response = openai.ChatCompletion.create(
        model="gpt-4-turbo",
        messages=[{"role": "system", "content":
prompt}],
        temperature=0.2,
        max_tokens=200
    )


    agent_reply =
response.choices[0].message.content.strip()
    update_memory(user_input, agent_reply)


    return agent_reply
```

Step 4: Autonomous Interaction Practically

Enable clear autonomous interaction explicitly (main.py):

python

```
from agent import generate_response


if __name__ == "__main__":
```

```python
    print("Context-Aware Customer Support Agent
(type 'exit' to quit)\n")


    while True:
        user_input = input("Customer: ")
        if user_input.lower() == "exit":
            break


        reply = generate_response(user_input)
        print("Agent:", reply, "\n")
```

Step 5: Testing, Logging, and Troubleshooting

Run and Test Clearly:

bash

```
python main.py
```

Example Interaction Explicitly:

vbnet

```
Customer: I can't access my account.

Agent: Please clearly verify your login details
first. If you're still unable to access, click cn
"Forgot Password" and follow the explicit
instructions to reset your credentials.


Customer: I already reset it, but still can't log
in.
```

Agent: Let me explicitly check your account details and investigate further. Please hold briefly while I confirm your account status clearly.

Customer: Okay, thanks.

Agent: You're welcome! I'll clearly get back to you shortly after reviewing your account status explicitly.

Practical Troubleshooting Advice

Clear, practical guidance explicitly:

Issue	Troubleshooting Advice Clearly
Memory not saving interactions	Verify file permissions and paths explicitly.
Weak responses from agent	Explicitly refine your CoT and Few-Shot prompts clearly.
Slow response time	Lower max_tokens explicitly or simplify prompt complexity.

Practical Enhancements

Clearly consider these practical improvements explicitly:

- **CRM Integration:** Access user-specific data explicitly to personalize responses.
- **Advanced escalation logic:** Automatically escalate unresolved or complex issues practically.
- **Persistent database storage:** Store and retrieve memory explicitly from databases like SQLite practically.

Best Practices Checklist

Explicitly follow practical guidelines clearly:

- Context and memory explicitly managed practically.
- Advanced prompt engineering explicitly implemented clearly.
- Clear autonomous interactions practically verified.
- Explicit logging and monitoring practically enabled.
- Robust error handling clearly and practically implemented.

Summary & Next Steps

In this practical, detailed project, you've explicitly learned to:

- Manage context and memory clearly for personalized interactions.
- Practically leverage advanced prompt engineering explicitly.
- Deliver autonomous, context-aware customer support practically.

You now have practical skills to build advanced, intelligent, and highly effective autonomous agents capable of delivering personalized and reliable customer experiences.

Chapter 6: Integrating Agents with External APIs and Tools

To unlock the full capabilities of autonomous agents, integrating them explicitly with **external APIs and tools** is essential. Such integration practically enables your agents to fetch real-time data, automate complex workflows, interact with databases, and perform tasks beyond standard language-model capabilities.

In this chapter, you'll practically learn clear, step-by-step methods for effectively integrating autonomous agents with popular external APIs, tools, and services, using OpenAI's SDK.

Why Integrate External APIs and Tools?

Clear practical benefits include:

- **Real-time Data:** Allow agents to fetch and use dynamic information practically.
- **Automation:** Automate external tasks explicitly (email sending, database updates).
- **Enhanced Functionality:** Significantly expand practical agent capabilities explicitly.

6.1 Introduction to External Integrations

Integrating autonomous agents explicitly with **external APIs and tools** significantly expands their capabilities. These integrations practically enable your agents to interact seamlessly with real-world systems, access dynamic data sources, automate processes, and provide richer, more intelligent interactions.

In this section, you'll clearly learn the foundational concepts of external integrations practically, understand key benefits explicitly, and explore common integration scenarios step-by-step.

What are External Integrations?

External integrations refer to practically connecting autonomous agents explicitly with third-party applications, services, databases, or APIs to:

- Retrieve or update real-time data explicitly.
- Automate workflows practically.
- Extend agent functionality clearly beyond built-in capabilities.

Key Benefits of External Integrations

Clear, practical benefits explicitly include:

Benefit	Practical Explanation Explicitly
Real-time Data Access	Agents clearly fetch dynamic information practically.
Enhanced Automation	Streamline complex tasks explicitly and efficiently practically.
Improved Decision-making	Access external information explicitly to enhance accuracy practically.
Integration with Existing Systems	Agents practically fit into existing technology workflows explicitly.

Common Types of External Integrations

Here's a clear of practical integration types explicitly:

Integration Type	Practical Examples Explicitly
REST APIs	Weather APIs, Payment Gateways, CRM Systems
Databases	SQL Databases (SQLite, PostgreSQL), NoSQL Databases (MongoDB)
Automation Platforms	Zapier, n8n, Make (formerly Integromat)
Messaging Platforms	Slack, Discord, Telegram

Examples of Real-World Integrations

Practical real-world scenarios clearly demonstrated explicitly:

Scenario	Practical Integration Clearly
Customer Support	Agents clearly integrate explicitly with CRM APIs practically to fetch customer data.
E-commerce	Autonomous order-tracking practically through shipping APIs explicitly.
Marketing Automation	Agents clearly trigger email campaigns practically via automation tools explicitly.

Understanding APIs (Application Programming Interfaces)

Clearly defined explicitly, an **API** is a practical interface explicitly allowing applications (including agents) to interact with external systems.

Practical components of APIs explicitly:

- **Endpoints:** URLs explicitly used to access resources practically.
- **Requests:** Practical operations explicitly (GET, POST, PUT, DELETE).
- **Responses:** Data explicitly returned practically from API calls (usually JSON).
- **Authentication:** Securely controlling explicit access practically via API keys or OAuth tokens.

Basic Example of API Integration (Practically Demonstrated):

Clearly demonstrate explicit API integration practically (e.g., fetching weather data):

```python
```

```
import requests
```

```python
def fetch_weather(city):
    api_key = "YOUR_WEATHER_API_KEY"
    url = f"https://api.openweathermap.org/data/2.5/weather?q={city}&appid={api_key}&units=metric"

    response = requests.get(url)
    if response.status_code == 200:
        data = response.json()
        return data
    else:
        return {"error": "Unable to fetch data explicitly."}


weather = fetch_weather("London")
print(weather)
```

Clear Practical Output:

```json
json

{
    "weather": [{"description": "clear sky"}],
    "main": {"temp": 20},
    "name": "London"
}
```

- **Security Considerations Clearly**
  Practical explicit considerations for security:
- **API Key Management:**
  Store API keys securely practically (e.g., environment variables explicitly).
- **Rate Limiting:**
  Clearly handle API rate limits explicitly by throttling requests practically.
- **Data Privacy:**
  Ensure compliance explicitly with data protection regulations practically.

Common Challenges and Practical Solutions

Clear explicit troubleshooting practically:

Challenge	Clear Practical Solution Explicitly
Authentication Errors	Explicitly verify API credentials practically.
API Rate Limits	Practically implement request throttling explicitly.
Data Formatting Issues	Validate and parse API responses clearly explicitly.

Tools and Libraries for Integrations

Practical tools explicitly recommended clearly:

- **Python Libraries:** `requests, aiohttp, httpx`
- **Automation Tools:** Zapier, n8n, Make
- **Databases:** SQLite, PostgreSQL, MongoDB

Best Practices Checklist for External Integrations

Clearly follow practical guidelines explicitly:

- Securely store and manage API keys explicitly.

- Clearly handle errors and exceptions practically.
- Explicitly validate and parse responses practically.
- Implement logging explicitly for monitoring practically.
- Practically test integrations thoroughly explicitly.

Summary & Next Steps

In this clear, practical section, you explicitly learned:

- Clearly understanding external integrations practically.
- Practical examples explicitly illustrating integrations.
- Explicit security and troubleshooting considerations clearly.

You're now ready practically and explicitly prepared to practically set up and implement external integrations step-by-step clearly.

6.2 Connecting to Web APIs (REST, GraphQL)

Web APIs allow your autonomous agents to access and interact with external systems practically, enhancing their capabilities significantly. In this section, you'll explicitly learn how to clearly connect your agents practically to the two most common types of Web APIs: **REST** and **GraphQL**.

You'll gain practical, step-by-step instructions clearly demonstrated through explicit examples.

Understanding REST and GraphQL APIs

REST APIs (Representational State Transfer)

Widely used, practical standard explicitly for API design.

Uses clear, predefined HTTP methods explicitly (GET, POST, PUT, DELETE).

Data format practically returned is typically JSON explicitly.

GraphQL APIs

- Clearly allows clients explicitly to request exactly the data needed practically.
- Single endpoint explicitly serving data practically based on queries.
- Flexible, precise, and practical for complex data retrieval explicitly.

Connecting to REST APIs Practically

Use Python's practical `requests` library explicitly to interact with REST APIs clearly.

Step-by-step REST API integration clearly:

Step 1: Install dependencies explicitly

bash

```
pip install requests python-dotenv
```

Step 2: Configure environment practically (`.env`)

ini

```
API_KEY="your-api-key-here"
```

Step 3: Practical REST API Request Explicitly

python

```
import requests
import os
from dotenv import load_dotenv

load_dotenv()
api_key = os.getenv("API_KEY")
```

```python
def fetch_data_rest(city):
    url = f"https://api.openweathermap.org/data/2.5/weather?q={city}&appid={api_key}&units=metric"

    response = requests.get(url)

    if response.status_code == 200:
        return response.json()
    else:
        return {"error": "Failed to retrieve data explicitly."}


weather_data = fetch_data_rest("London")
print(weather_data)
```

Clear Practical Output:

```json
{
  "weather": [{"description": "clear sky"}],
  "main": {"temp": 22},
  "name": "London"
}
```

Connecting to GraphQL APIs Practically

Explicitly interact practically with GraphQL APIs clearly using the same `requests` library.

Step-by-step GraphQL integration explicitly:

Step 1: Install dependencies practically

bash

```
pip install requests python-dotenv
```

Step 2: GraphQL Request Practically and Explicitly

python

```
import requests

def fetch_data_graphql():
    url = "https://countries.trevorblades.com/"
    query = """
    {
      country(code: "US") {
        name
        capital
        currency
      }
    }
    """
    response = requests.post(url, json={"query":
query})

    if response.status_code == 200:
        return response.json()
```

```
    else:
        return {"error": "Failed to retrieve data
explicitly."}


country_data = fetch_data_graphql()

print(country_data)
```

Clear Practical Output:

```json
{

  "data": {

    "country": {

      "name": "United States",

      "capital": "Washington D.C.",

      "currency": "USD"

    }

  }

}
```

Practical Differences between REST and GraphQL Explicitly

Clearly outlined explicitly differences practically:

Aspect	REST APIs Practically	GraphQL APIs Practically
Data Retrieval	Clearly fixed data sets explicitly.	Explicitly flexible and precise practically.
Endpoints	Multiple endpoints practically.	Single endpoint explicitly.

Aspect	REST APIs Practically	GraphQL APIs Practically
Performance	May result practically in over-fetching data explicitly.	Avoids practically over-fetching explicitly.

Handling Authentication Clearly

Practical explicit methods for authenticating clearly:

REST API Authentication explicitly (API Keys):

python

```python
headers = {"Authorization": f"Bearer {api_key}"}
response = requests.get(url, headers=headers)
```

GraphQL Authentication explicitly (API Tokens):

python

```python
headers = {"Authorization": "Bearer your_token_here"}
response = requests.post(url, json={"query": query}, headers=headers)
```

Error Handling Practically and Explicitly

Explicitly handle practical API errors clearly:

python

```python
def safe_api_request(url, method="GET", data=None, headers=None):
    try:
```

```python
        if method == "GET":
            response = requests.get(url,
headers=headers, timeout=10)
        elif method == "POST":
            response = requests.post(url,
json=data, headers=headers, timeout=10)

        response.raise_for_status()

        return response.json()

    except requests.exceptions.RequestException as
e:
        return {"error": str(e)}


result =
safe_api_request("https://api.example.com/data")
print(result)
```

Best Practices for API Integrations Clearly

Clear practical checklist explicitly:

- Use secure storage explicitly for API keys practically.
- Implement clear error handling explicitly.
- Practically validate API responses explicitly.
- Set explicit timeout practically for API calls clearly.
- Test integrations practically and explicitly in various scenarios.

Common Practical Issues and Explicit Solutions

Clear explicit troubleshooting practically:

Issue	Clear Practical Solution Explicitly
Authentication Errors	Explicitly verify your API credentials clearly.
Data Not Received Correctly	Validate API responses explicitly and practically clearly.
Timeouts or Slow Responses	Practically set explicit request timeouts clearly.

Practical Project Suggestion Clearly

REST: Practically build a real-time weather agent explicitly.

GraphQL: Create an agent clearly fetching country-specific information practically.

Summary & Next Steps

In this clear, practical section, you've explicitly learned:

- Clearly connecting practically to REST and GraphQL APIs explicitly.
- Explicit authentication handling and practical error management clearly.
- Practical explicit examples demonstrating both API types clearly.

You're now explicitly prepared to integrate these APIs practically with autonomous agents, significantly enhancing their capabilities explicitly.

6.3 Database Integration (SQL, NoSQL)

Integrating autonomous agents explicitly with databases (both **SQL** and **NoSQL**) practically enhances their capabilities significantly. This allows agents to store, manage, and retrieve data efficiently, maintain long-term context explicitly, and interact dynamically with structured and unstructured data practically.

In this practical section, you'll clearly learn explicit methods for integrating your agents practically with **SQL databases (SQLite)** and **NoSQL databases (MongoDB)** step-by-step.

Understanding SQL vs. NoSQL

Clear explicit differences practically explained:

Aspect	SQL Databases Practically	NoSQL Databases Practically
Structure	Tabular and relational explicitly	Flexible, document-based practically
Schema	Clearly defined schemas explicitly	Schema-less explicitly practical
Use-Cases	Structured data, relationships clearly	Unstructured data, flexible needs practically

---

SQL Integration Practically (SQLite)

Step-by-step guide explicitly:

Step 1: Install SQLite practically

bash

```
pip install sqlite3
```

Step 2: Create and Connect Database explicitly

python

```
import sqlite3
```

```python
def create_db():
    conn = sqlite3.connect('agent.db')
    cursor = conn.cursor()
    cursor.execute('''
        CREATE TABLE IF NOT EXISTS users (
            id INTEGER PRIMARY KEY,
            name TEXT,
            email TEXT UNIQUE
        )
    ''')
    conn.commit()
    conn.close()


create_db()
```

Step 3: Practical CRUD Operations explicitly

Create Data explicitly:

python

```python
def add_user(name, email):
    conn = sqlite3.connect('agent.db')
    cursor = conn.cursor()
    cursor.execute("INSERT INTO users (name, email) VALUES (?, ?)", (name, email))
    conn.commit()
    conn.close()
```

```python
add_user("John Doe", "john@example.com")
```

Read Data clearly:

python

```python
def get_users():
    conn = sqlite3.connect('agent.db')
    cursor = conn.cursor()
    cursor.execute("SELECT * FROM users")
    users = cursor.fetchall()
    conn.close()
    return users


print(get_users())
```

Clear Practical Output:

bash

```
[(1, 'John Doe', 'john@example.com')]
```

NoSQL Integration Practically (MongoDB)

MongoDB explicitly handles unstructured or semi-structured data practically, making it ideal for flexible use-cases explicitly.

Step-by-step guide explicitly:

Step 1: Install MongoDB driver explicitly

bash

```
pip install pymongo
```

Step 2: Connect explicitly and create Database practically

python

```python
from pymongo import MongoClient

def connect_db():
    client = MongoClient("mongodb://localhost:27017/")
    db = client["agentdb"]
    return db

db = connect_db()
```

Step 3: Practical CRUD Operations explicitly

Create Data explicitly:

python

```python
def add_user_mongo(name, email):
    users_collection = db["users"]
    user = {"name": name, "email": email}
    users_collection.insert_one(user)

add_user_mongo("Jane Smith", "jane@example.com")
```

Read Data practically:

python

```python
def get_users_mongo():
```

```python
    users_collection = db["users"]

    users = list(users_collection.find({}, {"_id":
0}))

    return users


print(get_users_mongo())
```

Clear Practical Output:

```json
json


[{"name": "Jane Smith", "email":
"jane@example.com"}]
```

Using Databases Practically with Autonomous Agents Explicitly

Practical explicit use-cases clearly:

- **Persistent Agent Memory explicitly:**
  Store user interactions practically, ensuring agents retain context explicitly.
- **Real-time Data Management clearly:**
  Practical integration for dynamic data retrieval explicitly and practically.

Example: Agent Memory with SQLite explicitly

Clearly demonstrate practical use explicitly:

```python
python


def store_interaction(user_msg, agent_response):

    conn = sqlite3.connect('agent.db')

    cursor = conn.cursor()
```

```
    cursor.execute('''

        CREATE TABLE IF NOT EXISTS interactions (

            id INTEGER PRIMARY KEY,

            user_message TEXT,

            agent_response TEXT

        )

    ''')

    cursor.execute('''

        INSERT INTO interactions (user_message,
agent_response)

        VALUES (?, ?)

    ''', (user_msg, agent_response))

    conn.commit()

    conn.close()


store_interaction("Hello", "Hi! How can I help?")
```

Example: Agent Memory with MongoDB explicitly

Clearly practical example explicitly:

```
python


def store_interaction_mongo(user_msg,
agent_response):

    interactions_collection = db["interactions"]

    interaction = {"user_message": user_msg,
"agent_response": agent_response}

    interactions_collection.insert_one(interaction)
```

```
store_interaction_mongo("Hello", "Hi! How can I
assist?")
```

Best Practices Checklist Clearly

Clear explicit checklist practically:

- Clearly choose appropriate database explicitly based on data needs practically.
- Secure database access explicitly practically.
- Implement explicit practical error handling clearly.
- Regularly backup data explicitly and practically.
- Clearly optimize database queries explicitly practically.

Common Issues and Explicit Solutions Practically

Clear practical troubleshooting explicitly:

Issue	Clear Practical Solution Explicitly
Connection errors	Verify database connection strings explicitly and practically.
Data Integrity Issues	Clearly implement unique constraints explicitly.
Slow queries	Explicitly index important fields practically.

Security Considerations Explicitly

Practical clear considerations explicitly:

- **Secure Credentials:**
  Store database credentials explicitly in environment variables practically.

- **Validation:**
  Clearly validate input data explicitly practically to prevent injection attacks.

Practical Project Suggestion Explicitly

- **SQLite:** Practically build an agent explicitly storing and retrieving user interactions clearly.
- **MongoDB:** Develop an agent clearly managing flexible user preferences practically.

Summary & Next Steps

In this clear, practical section, you explicitly learned:

- Practically integrating autonomous agents explicitly with SQL and NoSQL databases.
- Explicitly performing CRUD operations practically clearly demonstrated.
- Practical explicit examples of storing agent memory clearly and explicitly.

You're now practically and explicitly prepared to use database integrations practically with autonomous agents, enabling powerful, context-aware interactions explicitly.

6.4 Integration with Productivity Tools (Slack, Email, Calendars)

Integrating autonomous agents explicitly with **productivity tools** such as **Slack**, **Email**, and **Calendars** practically enhances their ability to automate workflows, improve communication, manage schedules, and increase overall efficiency clearly and explicitly.

In this practical section, you'll clearly learn step-by-step how to explicitly integrate your agents practically with these essential productivity tools.

Why Integrate with Productivity Tools?

Clear practical benefits explicitly include:

- **Enhanced Communication:** Automate messaging practically via Slack and email explicitly.
- **Scheduling Automation:** Practically manage events and reminders explicitly using calendars.
- **Workflow Automation:** Clearly streamline tasks practically, reducing manual effort explicitly.

Slack Integration Practically and Explicitly

Integrating your agent with **Slack** clearly allows automated messaging, alerts, and notifications practically.

◆ Step-by-Step Slack Integration explicitly:

Step 1: Setup explicitly

Create a Slack App practically at api.slack.com/apps.

Obtain your Slack **Bot Token** clearly.

Step 2: Install Slack SDK explicitly

bash

```
pip install slack_sdk python-dotenv
```

Step 3: Explicitly Send Slack Messages Practically

python

```
from slack_sdk import WebClient
import os
from dotenv import load_dotenv
```

```python
load_dotenv()

SLACK_BOT_TOKEN = os.getenv("SLACK_BOT_TOKEN")


client = WebClient(token=SLACK_BOT_TOKEN)


def send_slack_message(channel, message):
    response =
client.chat_postMessage(channel=channel,
text=message)

    return response


send_slack_message("#general", "Hello from your
autonomous agent explicitly!")
```

Clear Practical Result:
A Slack message sent practically by the agent explicitly to the specified channel clearly.

Email Integration Practically and Explicitly

Agents clearly send emails explicitly using Python's SMTP integration practically.

◆ **Step-by-Step Email Integration explicitly:**

Step 1: Setup explicitly
Use an email provider explicitly like Gmail (SMTP credentials practically).

Step 2: Python Email setup explicitly

```bash
bash
```

```bash
pip install python-dotenv
```

Step 3: Explicitly Send Emails Practically

python

```python
import smtplib, ssl
from email.mime.text import MIMEText
from email.mime.multipart import MIMEMultipart
import os
from dotenv import load_dotenv

load_dotenv()

smtp_server = "smtp.gmail.com"
port = 465
sender_email = os.getenv("EMAIL_ADDRESS")
password = os.getenv("EMAIL_PASSWORD")

def send_email(receiver_email, subject, body):
    message = MIMEMultipart()
    message["From"] = sender_email
    message["To"] = receiver_email
    message["Subject"] = subject
    message.attach(MIMEText(body, "plain"))

    context = ssl.create_default_context()
    with smtplib.SMTP_SSL(smtp_server, port, context=context) as server:
```

```
        server.login(sender_email, password)

        server.sendmail(sender_email,
receiver_email, message.as_string())
```

```
send_email("recipient@example.com", "Test Email",
"Hello from your autonomous agent explicitly!")
```

Clear Practical Result:

The email explicitly arrives practically in the recipient's inbox clearly.

Calendar Integration Practically and Explicitly

Practically integrate your agent explicitly with Google Calendar using its API.

◆ **Step-by-Step Calendar Integration explicitly:**

Step 1: Google API Setup explicitly

Set up your project practically at Google Developers Console.

Enable Google Calendar API explicitly and download your credentials JSON practically.

Step 2: Install dependencies explicitly

```bash
```

```
pip install google-auth google-auth-oauthlib
google-auth-httplib2 google-api-python-client
```

Step 3: Add Calendar Events explicitly practically

```python
```

```
from google.oauth2 import service_account

from googleapiclient.discovery import build
```

```python
SCOPES =
['https://www.googleapis.com/auth/calendar']

SERVICE_ACCOUNT_FILE = 'credentials.json'


credentials =
service_account.Credentials.from_service_account_fi
le(
    SERVICE_ACCOUNT_FILE, scopes=SCOPES)


service = build('calendar', 'v3',
credentials=credentials)


def create_calendar_event():
    event = {
        'summary': 'Autonomous Agent Meeting',
        'start': {'dateTime': '2024-06-15T10:00:00',
'timeZone': 'UTC'},
        'end': {'dateTime': '2024-06-15T11:00:00',
'timeZone': 'UTC'},
    }


    event =
service.events().insert(calendarId='primary',
body=event).execute()
    print('Event created explicitly:',
event.get('htmlLink'))


create_calendar_event()
```

Clear Practical Result:
An event explicitly appears practically on your Google Calendar clearly.

Best Practices Checklist Explicitly

Clear explicit checklist practically:

- Securely manage credentials explicitly using `.env`.
- Handle API errors explicitly and practically.
- Validate and clearly test integrations explicitly.
- Maintain clear explicit logging practically.
- Monitor API usage practically and explicitly.

Common Issues and Explicit Solutions

Clear practical troubleshooting explicitly:

Issue	Clear Practical Solution Explicitly
Slack Authentication Issues	Explicitly verify Slack tokens practically.
Email Sending Failures	Explicitly confirm SMTP server details practically.
Calendar Event Errors	Practically confirm Google Calendar permissions explicitly.

Security Considerations Explicitly

- **Credential Storage:**
  Explicitly use environment variables practically to store credentials securely clearly.
- **Permission Management:**
  Practically restrict API permissions explicitly to essential access clearly.

Practical Project Suggestion Explicitly

- **Slack:** Practically build an agent explicitly sending project alerts clearly.
- **Email:** Explicitly automate weekly status emails practically.
- **Calendar:** Practically automate event scheduling explicitly from agent tasks clearly.

Summary & Next Steps

In this practical, explicit section, you've clearly learned:

- Explicitly integrating autonomous agents practically with Slack, Email, and Calendars.
- Practical explicit implementations clearly demonstrated step-by-step.
- Best practices explicitly for robust integration practically and clearly.

You're now explicitly prepared practically to enhance your agents by automating productivity and communication workflows clearly.

6.5 Practical Project: Autonomous Data Analyst Agent

In this hands-on, practical project, you'll build an **Autonomous Data Analyst Agent** explicitly capable of fetching, analyzing, and reporting data autonomously. The agent integrates practically with web APIs, databases, and productivity tools (Slack or Email) to deliver insightful analyses and automated reports clearly and explicitly.

Project Explicitly

Goal Practically:

- Develop an autonomous agent explicitly capable of:
- Fetching real-time data practically from REST APIs.
- Storing and managing data explicitly in a database (SQLite).
- Performing practical data analysis explicitly using OpenAI's language models.
- Sending analysis reports explicitly via Slack or Email.

173

Real-world Relevance Explicitly:

This agent practically automates data analysis, improving decision-making efficiency clearly and explicitly across businesses.

Step-by-Step Project Guide Practically and Explicitly

Follow these explicit practical steps clearly:

Step	Clearly Defined Stage	Practical Explanation Clearly
1	Set Up Project Environment explicitly	Explicitly install dependencies and environment.
2	Fetch Data Explicitly from a REST API	Practically retrieve data explicitly.
3	Store Data Practically in Database (SQLite)	Clearly implement data storage explicitly.
4	Perform Autonomous Data Analysis Clearly	Practical analysis explicitly using OpenAI.
5	Generate and Send Reports explicitly	Practically deliver insights explicitly via Slack/Email.

Step 1: Set Up Project Environment Explicitly

Create your environment practically:

bash

```
mkdir data-analyst-agent

cd data-analyst-agent

python -m venv env

source env/bin/activate # macOS/Linux

.\env\Scripts\activate  # Windows
```

174

```
pip install requests sqlite3 openai slack_sdk
python-dotenv
```

Configure `.env` explicitly:

```ini
OPENAI_API_KEY="your-openai-key"

SLACK_BOT_TOKEN="your-slack-token"
```

Step 2: Fetch Data Explicitly from REST API

Practical example explicitly fetching cryptocurrency data:

```python
import requests


def fetch_crypto_prices():
    url =
"https://api.coingecko.com/api/v3/simple/price?ids=
bitcoin,ethereum&vs_currencies=usd"
    response = requests.get(url)
    if response.status_code == 200:
        return response.json()
    else:
        return {}


prices = fetch_crypto_prices()
print(prices)
```

Clear Practical Output:

json

```json
{"bitcoin": {"usd": 65000}, "ethereum": {"usd":
3500}}
```

Step 3: Store Data Practically in SQLite Database

Explicitly store fetched data practically:

python

```python
import sqlite3


def create_db():
    conn = sqlite3.connect('crypto_prices.db')
    cursor = conn.cursor()
    cursor.execute('''
        CREATE TABLE IF NOT EXISTS prices (
            id INTEGER PRIMARY KEY AUTOINCREMENT,
            crypto TEXT,
            price REAL
        )
    ''')
    conn.commit()
    conn.close()


def store_prices(data):
```

```
    conn = sqlite3.connect('crypto_prices.db')

    cursor = conn.cursor()

    for crypto, info in data.items():

        cursor.execute('INSERT INTO prices (crypto,
price) VALUES (?, ?)', (crypto, info['usd']))

    conn.commit()

    conn.close()


create_db()

store_prices(prices)
```

Step 4: Perform Autonomous Data Analysis Explicitly

Practically analyze data explicitly using OpenAI:

```python
import openai

import os

from dotenv import load_dotenv


load_dotenv()

openai.api_key = os.getenv("OPENAI_API_KEY")


def analyze_data():

    conn = sqlite3.connect('crypto_prices.db')

    cursor = conn.cursor()
```

```python
    cursor.execute('SELECT crypto, price FROM
prices')

    rows = cursor.fetchall()

    conn.close()


    data_summary = "\n".join([f"{crypto}: ${price}"
for crypto, price in rows])


    prompt = f"""
    You are an autonomous data analyst agent.


    Analyze the latest cryptocurrency prices
explicitly provided:
    {data_summary}


    Provide a brief insightful summary clearly.
    """


    response = openai.ChatCompletion.create(
        model="gpt-4-turbo",
        messages=[{"role": "system", "content":
prompt}],
        temperature=0.3,
        max_tokens=200
    )
```

```python
    return
response.choices[0].message.content.strip()


report = analyze_data()

print(report)
```

Clear Practical Example Output:

```swift


Bitcoin is currently priced at $65,000, while
Ethereum stands at $3,500. Bitcoin maintains strong
growth, reflecting positive market confidence,
whereas Ethereum offers opportunities for
diversification.
```

Step 5: Generate and Send Reports Explicitly via Slack

Practically deliver reports explicitly through Slack:

```python


from slack_sdk import WebClient


SLACK_BOT_TOKEN = os.getenv("SLACK_BOT_TOKEN")

client = WebClient(token=SLACK_BOT_TOKEN)


def send_report_slack(channel, message):
    client.chat_postMessage(channel=channel,
text=message)


send_report_slack("#analytics", report)
```

Clear Practical Result:

The analysis explicitly appears practically in the Slack channel clearly.

Alternative: Send Reports Explicitly via Email

Alternatively, explicitly use email practically for reports:

python

```python
import smtplib, ssl
from email.mime.text import MIMEText
from email.mime.multipart import MIMEMultipart

smtp_server = "smtp.gmail.com"
port = 465
sender_email = os.getenv("EMAIL_ADDRESS")
password = os.getenv("EMAIL_PASSWORD")

def send_email(receiver_email, subject, body):
    message = MIMEMultipart()
    message["From"] = sender_email
    message["To"] = receiver_email
    message["Subject"] = subject
    message.attach(MIMEText(body, "plain"))

    context = ssl.create_default_context()
    with smtplib.SMTP_SSL(smtp_server, port,
context=context) as server:
        server.login(sender_email, password)
```

```
        server.sendmail(sender_email,
receiver_email, message.as_string())


send_email("recipient@example.com", "Crypto Market
Report", report)
```

Best Practices Checklist Explicitly

Clear explicit checklist practically:

- Secure API keys explicitly.
- Clearly manage database connections practically.
- Implement explicit error handling clearly.
- Verify and practically test integration explicitly.
- Explicitly log interactions practically.

Common Issues and Explicit Solutions

Clear practical troubleshooting explicitly:

Issue	Clear Practical Solution Explicitly
API Data Errors	Verify REST API endpoints explicitly.
Database Connection Failures	Check database connections explicitly practically.
Slack or Email Delivery Issues	Verify credentials explicitly and practically.

Practical Enhancements Explicitly

Automate scheduled reporting explicitly using Cron Jobs practically.

Integrate with visualization tools explicitly for detailed insights practically.

Summary & Next Steps

In this clear, practical project, you've explicitly learned:

- Practically integrating autonomous agents explicitly with APIs, databases, and productivity tools.
- Autonomous practical data analysis explicitly using OpenAI.
- Automated clear reporting explicitly delivered practically.

You now possess practical explicit skills to build sophisticated, autonomous data analyst agents explicitly capable of performing advanced data tasks clearly.

Chapter 7: Designing and Managing Autonomous Workflows

Autonomous workflows explicitly empower agents to manage multiple tasks clearly, coordinate interactions practically, and achieve complex goals autonomously. This chapter practically guides you through explicitly designing, building, and managing robust autonomous workflows clearly and practically using OpenAI's Agents SDK.

Why Autonomous Workflows?

Clear explicit advantages practically include:

- **Efficiency:** Automate complex, repetitive tasks explicitly.
- **Scalability:** Handle increased workloads practically with minimal human oversight.
- **Adaptability:** Quickly respond explicitly to changing conditions practically.

7.1 Autonomous Workflow Fundamentals

Autonomous workflows explicitly empower agents to handle multiple, interconnected tasks practically without constant human supervision. In this section, you'll clearly learn practical fundamentals for designing and implementing effective autonomous workflows explicitly, preparing you to orchestrate sophisticated autonomous systems practically.

What is an Autonomous Workflow?

An **autonomous workflow** is explicitly a series of clearly defined tasks practically executed autonomously by agents. Each task within the workflow is practically managed by specialized agents explicitly designed to handle distinct roles, communicate, coordinate, and dynamically adapt clearly to conditions.

Benefits of Autonomous Workflows Practically and Explicitly

Clear explicit benefits practically:

Benefit	Practical Explanation Explicitly
Efficiency and Speed	Automate clearly and execute tasks rapidly explicitly.
Reduced Errors	Minimize human errors explicitly through automated processes practically.
Scalability and Flexibility	Adapt and expand workflows explicitly with minimal human input practically.
Improved Productivity	Automate repetitive tasks explicitly, freeing human resources practically.

Core Components of Autonomous Workflows Explicitly

Clear explicit practical components:

Component	Explicit Practical Explanation
Agents	Autonomous entities explicitly performing specific tasks practically.
Tasks	Clearly defined explicit units of work executed practically.
Communication	Explicit structured protocols clearly enabling agent coordination practically.
Orchestration	Practically coordinating and sequencing tasks explicitly.
Error Handling	Clear explicit recovery mechanisms for robust operation practically.

Designing Autonomous Workflows Explicitly and Practically

Clearly follow these explicit practical design principles:

◆ **Modularity Practically:**

Explicitly divide workflows clearly into discrete, manageable tasks practically.

Easier practical debugging explicitly and clearly facilitates scalability.

◆ **Clear Responsibility Explicitly:**

Clearly define explicit roles for each agent practically.

Ensures practical accountability explicitly and reduces confusion clearly.

◆ **Structured Communication Explicitly:**

Use explicit structured formats clearly (e.g., JSON practically) for agent interaction explicitly.

Reduces practical miscommunication explicitly clearly.

◆ **Error Resilience Practically:**

Explicitly plan practical recovery strategies clearly for potential failures explicitly.

Maintain explicit robust operation clearly practically.

Practical Example of Workflow Design Explicitly

Consider a clearly structured **autonomous customer onboarding workflow** practically:

Step	Task Clearly Defined	Agent Practically Responsible Explicitly
1	Receive Customer Request explicitly	Intake Agent practically.
2	Validate Customer Data clearly	Validation Agent explicitly practically.
3	Create Account explicitly	Account Management Agent clearly practically.

185

Step	Task Clearly Defined	Agent Practically Responsible Explicitly
4	Send Welcome Email explicitly	Email Notification Agent practically explicitly.
5	Follow-up practically	Customer Support Agent clearly explicitly.

Implementing Workflow Orchestration Practically Explicitly

Simple Python orchestration clearly demonstrated explicitly:

python

```python
def onboarding_workflow(customer_data):
    tasks = [
        ("Intake Agent", "Receive Customer Request"),
        ("Validation Agent", "Validate Customer Data"),
        ("Account Agent", "Create Account"),
        ("Email Agent", "Send Welcome Email"),
        ("Support Agent", "Follow-up")
    ]

    for agent, task in tasks:
        print(f"{agent} explicitly executing: {task}")
        # Explicit practical logic for task execution here
```

```
onboarding_workflow({"name": "John Doe", "email":
"john@example.com"})
```

Handling Errors in Autonomous Workflows Explicitly

Practical error handling clearly demonstrated explicitly:

python

```python
def execute_task(agent, task):
    try:
        print(f"{agent} explicitly starting:
{task}")
        # Practical explicit task execution logic
here
    except Exception as e:
        print(f"Error explicitly in {task}: {e}")
        handle_recovery(agent, task)


def handle_recovery(agent, task):
    print(f"Recovery explicitly initiated
practically for {task} by {agent}")
```

Monitoring and Logging Explicitly and Practically

Clear explicit logging practically implemented:

python

```python
import logging
```

```
logging.basicConfig(filename='workflow.log',
level=logging.INFO)


def execute_task(agent, task):

    logging.info(f"{agent} explicitly started:
{task}")

    # Explicit practical task logic

    logging.info(f"{agent} explicitly completed:
{task}")


execute_task("Account Agent", "Create Account")
```

Best Practices Checklist Explicitly

Clear explicit practical checklist:

- Modularize workflows explicitly practically.
- Define explicit clear roles practically for each agent.
- Establish structured communication explicitly practically.
- Implement robust error handling explicitly clearly.
- Monitor and log explicitly practically every workflow step.

Common Issues and Explicit Solutions Practically

Clear practical troubleshooting explicitly:

Issue	Clear Practical Solution Explicitly
Task Overlap	Explicitly define agent responsibilities practically.
Poor Communication	Use structured JSON messaging explicitly practically.
Workflow Failures	Explicitly implement error handling practically clearly.

Security Considerations Explicitly

Data Security:
Explicitly handle sensitive data securely practically.

Secure Communication:
Clearly use encrypted protocols explicitly practically for agent communication.

Practical Enhancements Explicitly

Implement dynamic adaptation practically based on real-time conditions explicitly.

Integrate explicit real-time monitoring dashboards practically.

Summary & Next Steps

In this clear practical section, you explicitly learned:

- Fundamentals of designing autonomous workflows explicitly practically.
- Practical explicit guidelines clearly demonstrated step-by-step.
- Robust error handling explicitly clearly and practical monitoring.

You're now practically equipped explicitly to build efficient, reliable autonomous workflows clearly, laying the foundation for advanced autonomous systems practically.

7.2 Designing Sequential and Parallel Workflows

In autonomous workflows, tasks can be structured explicitly either **sequentially** (tasks executed clearly one after another) or **in parallel** (tasks executed simultaneously practically). Understanding explicitly how and when to use these two workflow types practically ensures efficient, scalable, and robust automation.

This section provides clear, step-by-step guidance practically for explicitly designing and implementing sequential and parallel workflows using OpenAI's Agents SDK.

Understanding Workflow Types Explicitly

◆ Sequential Workflow:

Tasks are executed clearly one after another explicitly.

Next task practically depends explicitly on completion of the previous task.

Ideal practically for tasks explicitly requiring ordered execution clearly.

◆ Parallel Workflow:

Tasks execute simultaneously explicitly.

Independent practical tasks explicitly that can be run concurrently.

Ideal explicitly for maximizing efficiency and reducing overall completion time practically.

When to Use Sequential vs. Parallel Explicitly

Workflow Type	Practical Scenarios Explicitly
Sequential	Data validation, task dependencies, ordered steps explicitly.
Parallel	Independent API calls, data fetching, concurrent analysis explicitly.

Designing Sequential Workflows Practically

Clearly define tasks explicitly in a practical sequence:

◆ Sequential Workflow Explicit Example:

python

```python
def sequential_workflow():
    tasks = [
        "fetch data explicitly",
        "validate data practically",
        "analyze data clearly",
        "generate report explicitly"
    ]

    for task in tasks:
        execute_task(task)

def execute_task(task):
    print(f"Executing explicitly: {task}")
    # Practical explicit task logic here

sequential_workflow()
```

Clear Practical Output Explicitly:

```yaml
Executing explicitly: fetch data explicitly
Executing explicitly: validate data practically
Executing explicitly: analyze data clearly
Executing explicitly: generate report explicitly
```

Designing Parallel Workflows Practically

Use Python's explicit threading clearly to implement parallel workflows practically:

◆ **Parallel Workflow Explicit Example:**

python

```python
import threading


def task(name):
    print(f"Starting explicitly: {name}")
    # Practical explicit logic here
    print(f"Completed explicitly: {name}")


tasks = ["fetch data A", "fetch data B", "fetch data C"]


threads = []
for t in tasks:
    thread = threading.Thread(target=task, args=(t,))
    threads.append(thread)
    thread.start()


for thread in threads:
    thread.join()


print("All parallel tasks explicitly completed.")
```

Clear Practical Output Explicitly:

sql

```
Starting explicitly: fetch data A
Starting explicitly: fetch data B
Starting explicitly: fetch data C
Completed explicitly: fetch data A
Completed explicitly: fetch data B
Completed explicitly: fetch data C
All parallel tasks explicitly completed.
```

Combining Sequential and Parallel Workflows Explicitly

Explicitly combine practical sequential and parallel workflows for complex scenarios clearly:

◆ **Practical Explicit Combination Example:**

python

```python
def combined_workflow():
    print("Starting explicit workflow practically")

    # Sequential Task
    execute_task("initial setup explicitly")

    # Parallel Tasks
    parallel_tasks = ["fetch data explicitly",
"load configurations practically"]
```

```
    threads =
[threading.Thread(target=execute_task, args=(t,))
for t in parallel_tasks]

    for thread in threads:

        thread.start()

    for thread in threads:

        thread.join()


    # Sequential Task

    execute_task("final analysis explicitly")


combined_workflow()
```

Best Practices Checklist Explicitly

Clear explicit practical checklist:

- Clearly identify explicit task dependencies practically.
- Explicitly use sequential workflows for dependent tasks practically.
- Implement parallel workflows explicitly for independent tasks clearly.
- Explicitly handle exceptions practically in each task clearly.
- Explicitly log clearly and monitor workflows practically.

Common Issues and Explicit Solutions

Clear practical troubleshooting explicitly:

Issue	Clear Practical Solution Explicitly
Tasks Overlapping Incorrectly	Clearly verify explicit dependencies practically.

Issue	Clear Practical Solution Explicitly
Slow Execution Sequentially	Move independent tasks explicitly to parallel execution practically.
Concurrency Errors Practically	Use explicit thread-safe operations clearly.

Practical Example: Autonomous Agent Workflow Explicitly

A practical explicit workflow combining sequential and parallel execution explicitly:

python

```
import threading

import time


def execute_task(task):

    print(f"Executing explicitly: {task}")

    time.sleep(1)  # Simulate practical explicit
task duration

    print(f"Completed explicitly: {task}")


def agent_workflow():

    print("Workflow explicitly starting
practically")


    # Sequential Task

    execute_task("Authenticate explicitly")
```

```python
# Parallel Data Fetching
data_tasks = ["Fetch customer data explicitly",
"Fetch product data practically"]

threads =
[threading.Thread(target=execute_task, args=(t,))
for t in data_tasks]

for thread in threads:
    thread.start()

for thread in threads:
    thread.join()


# Sequential Task
execute_task("Analyze data clearly")


# Parallel Reporting
report_tasks = ["Generate PDF report
explicitly", "Send email notification practically"]

threads =
[threading.Thread(target=execute_task, args=(t,))
for t in report_tasks]

for thread in threads:
    thread.start()

for thread in threads:
    thread.join()


print("Workflow explicitly completed
practically")
```

```
agent_workflow()
```

Security Considerations Explicitly

Thread Safety:
Ensure shared resources explicitly managed practically using thread-safe operations clearly.

Data Integrity:
Validate data explicitly clearly between sequential tasks practically.

Practical Enhancements Explicitly

Async Execution: Use asynchronous execution explicitly (`asyncio`) practically.

Dynamic Workflow Management: Implement dynamic adjustments explicitly practically based on runtime conditions.

Summary & Next Steps

In this practical, explicit section, you've clearly learned:

- Explicitly designing sequential and parallel workflows practically.
- Practical explicit implementations clearly demonstrated step-by-step.
- Combining both workflow types explicitly practically.

You're now explicitly and practically equipped to design and implement complex autonomous workflows clearly, enhancing your automation capabilities explicitly.

7.3 Handling Workflow Errors and Exceptions

Robust **error handling and exception management** explicitly ensure your autonomous workflows run reliably practically, recovering gracefully from failures clearly. Properly managing workflow errors explicitly is essential to maintain reliability, trust, and performance practically in your agent-based systems.

In this practical section, you'll clearly learn step-by-step how to explicitly implement robust error handling practically within autonomous workflows using OpenAI's Agents SDK.

Why Handle Workflow Errors Explicitly?

Clear explicit benefits practically:

- **Reliability:** Ensure workflows practically continue despite explicit errors clearly.
- **Transparency:** Clearly log explicit failures practically for easier troubleshooting.
- **Improved User Experience:** Explicitly provide practical graceful failure handling clearly.

Common Workflow Errors Practically

Explicitly common practical errors clearly include:

Error Type	Explicit Practical Description
Network/API Errors	Failed API calls explicitly practically.
Database Errors	Connection or transaction issues explicitly practically.
Logic Errors	Incorrect task sequencing explicitly practically.
Unexpected Exceptions	Unhandled errors explicitly practically.

Implementing Error Handling Explicitly and Practically

Explicitly implement clear practical exception handling using Python's `try-except` explicitly:

◆ **Basic Explicit Error Handling Example:**

```
python
```

```python
def execute_task(task):

    try:

        print(f"Executing explicitly: {task}")

        # Explicit practical logic

    except Exception as e:

        print(f"Error explicitly in task '{task}':
{e}")


execute_task("fetch data explicitly")
```

Advanced Error Handling Practically Explicitly

Explicitly implement clear practical detailed error handling:

python

```python
def safe_task_execution(task_func, task_name):

    try:

        task_func()

        print(f"Task '{task_name}' explicitly
completed successfully practically.")

    except ConnectionError as ce:

        handle_connection_error(task_name, ce)

    except ValueError as ve:

        handle_validation_error(task_name, ve)

    except Exception as e:

        handle_generic_error(task_name, e)
```

```python
def handle_connection_error(task, error):
    print(f"Connection error explicitly in
'{task}': {error}. Retrying practically...")


def handle_validation_error(task, error):
    print(f"Validation error explicitly in
'{task}': {error}. Skipping task clearly.")


def handle_generic_error(task, error):
    print(f"Unhandled error explicitly in '{task}':
{error}. Logging clearly.")


safe_task_execution(lambda: 1/0, "Data Analysis
explicitly")
```

Clear Practical Output Explicitly:

```
nginx
```

```
Unhandled error explicitly in 'Data Analysis
explicitly': division by zero. Logging clearly.
```

Retry Mechanisms Practically and Explicitly

Explicitly handle transient errors clearly practically by retrying tasks
explicitly:

```
python
```

```
import time
```

```python
def retry_task(task_func, retries=3, delay=2):
    attempt = 0
    while attempt < retries:
        try:
            task_func()
            print("Task explicitly succeeded practically.")
            break
        except Exception as e:
            attempt += 1
            print(f"Attempt {attempt} explicitly failed practically: {e}")
            if attempt < retries:
                print(f"Retrying explicitly after {delay} seconds practically.")
                time.sleep(delay)
            else:
                print("Task explicitly failed practically after maximum retries.")


retry_task(lambda: 1/0)
```

Logging Errors Explicitly and Practically

Practical explicit logging clearly demonstrated:

python


```python
import logging
```

```python
logging.basicConfig(filename='workflow_errors.log',
level=logging.ERROR)


def execute_logged_task(task_func, task_name):

    try:

        task_func()

    except Exception as e:

        logging.error(f"Task '{task_name}'
explicitly failed practically: {e}")


execute_logged_task(lambda:
open("nonexistent.txt"), "Open File explicitly")
```

Logged Explicit Practical Output:

```ruby
ERROR:root:Task 'Open File explicitly' explicitly
failed practically: [Errno 2] No such file or
directory: 'nonexistent.txt'
```

Best Practices Checklist Explicitly

Clear explicit practical checklist:

- Explicitly handle anticipated errors practically.
- Clearly implement retry mechanisms explicitly.
- Explicitly log practical errors clearly.
- Implement practical fallback or recovery strategies explicitly.
- Test error handling explicitly thoroughly practically.

Common Issues and Explicit Solutions Practically

Clear practical troubleshooting explicitly:

Issue	Clear Practical Solution Explicitly
Unhandled Exceptions	Explicitly use broad try-except blocks practically.
Silent Failures	Explicitly implement detailed logging practically clearly.
Repeated Failures Practically	Clearly implement retry limits explicitly practically.

Security Considerations Explicitly

Avoid explicit logging of sensitive information practically.

Use explicit secure channels practically for error notifications clearly.

Practical Project Example: Robust Autonomous Workflow Explicitly

Explicit practical autonomous workflow clearly handling errors explicitly:

python

```python
import logging, time
logging.basicConfig(filename='robust_workflow.log',
level=logging.INFO)


def fetch_data():
    raise ConnectionError("API unavailable
explicitly.")


def analyze_data():
    print("Analyzing data explicitly practically.")
```

```python
def workflow():

    tasks = [("Fetch Data explicitly", fetch_data),
("Analyze Data practically", analyze_data)]

    for task_name, task_func in tasks:

        try:

            task_func()

            logging.info(f"Task '{task_name}'
explicitly succeeded practically.")

        except Exception as e:

            logging.error(f"Task '{task_name}'
explicitly failed practically: {e}")

            handle_recovery(task_name)


def handle_recovery(task_name):

    print(f"Recovery explicitly initiated
practically for '{task_name}'.")


workflow()
```

Clear Practical Output Explicitly:

```kotlin


Recovery explicitly initiated practically for
'Fetch Data explicitly'.

Analyzing data explicitly practically.
```

Practical Enhancements Explicitly

Alert Systems: Explicitly notify via Slack or Email practically upon errors.

Dashboard Monitoring: Practically visualize explicit errors and recoveries clearly.

Summary & Next Steps

In this practical, explicit section, you clearly learned:

- Explicitly handling workflow errors practically.
- Practical explicit implementations clearly demonstrated step-by-step.
- Best practices explicitly for robust workflows practically.

You're now explicitly and practically equipped to build reliable autonomous workflows clearly, gracefully handling errors explicitly and practically ensuring robust system performance.

7.4 Monitoring and Observability

Effective **monitoring and observability** explicitly ensures autonomous workflows run reliably practically, providing clear visibility into the performance, health, and behavior of agents. By practically implementing monitoring and logging explicitly, you proactively identify, diagnose, and resolve issues clearly.

In this practical section, you'll explicitly learn clear, step-by-step methods for implementing robust monitoring and observability practically within your OpenAI autonomous agent workflows.

Why Monitoring and Observability Matter Explicitly

Clear explicit practical benefits include:

Rapid Issue Detection: Quickly identify explicit practical problems.

Enhanced Reliability: Maintain clear explicit workflow performance practically.

Improved Transparency: Clearly understand explicit agent behaviors practically.

Better Decision-making: Use explicit data practically for workflow improvements.

Key Concepts in Monitoring and Observability Explicitly

Concept Practical Explanation Explicitly

Logging Record explicit events practically for troubleshooting clearly.

Metrics Measure explicit workflow performance practically (speed, errors).

Tracing Track explicit execution flow practically across tasks clearly.

Alerts Notify explicitly practically when issues occur clearly.

Implementing Practical Logging Explicitly

Clearly implement practical structured logging explicitly using Python's logging module:

python

```
import logging


logging.basicConfig(
    filename='workflow.log',
    level=logging.INFO,
    format='%(asctime)s - %(levelname)s -
%(message)s'
)


def execute_task(task_name):
```

```
    logging.info(f"Task explicitly started
practically: {task_name}")

    try:

        # Explicit practical task logic

        logging.info(f"Task explicitly completed
successfully practically: {task_name}")

    except Exception as e:

        logging.error(f"Task '{task_name}'
explicitly failed practically: {e}")


execute_task("Data Fetch explicitly")
```

Collecting and Using Metrics Practically Explicitly

Practically measure explicit workflow metrics clearly:

python

```
import time


task_metrics = {}


def execute_timed_task(task_name, task_func):
    start_time = time.time()
    try:
        task_func()
        success = True
    except Exception:
        success = False
```

```python
    end_time = time.time()

    task_metrics[task_name] = {
        "duration": end_time - start_time,
        "success": success
    }


execute_timed_task("Sample Task explicitly",
lambda: time.sleep(2))
print(task_metrics)
```

Clear Practical Output Explicitly:

```json
json


{"Sample Task explicitly": {"duration": 2.0,
"success": true}}
```

Tracing Workflow Execution Explicitly Practically

Explicitly track workflow tasks practically:

```python
python


workflow_trace = []


def execute_traced_task(task_name):
    workflow_trace.append({"task": task_name,
"status": "started"})
    try:
        # Explicit practical task logic here
```

```
        workflow_trace.append({"task": task_name,
"status": "completed"})

    except Exception as e:

        workflow_trace.append({"task": task_name,
"status": f"failed: {e}"})


execute_traced_task("Task A explicitly")

print(workflow_trace)
```

Clear Practical Output Explicitly:

```json

[

  {"task": "Task A explicitly", "status":
"started"},

  {"task": "Task A explicitly", "status":
"completed"}

]
```

Setting Up Alerts Practically and Explicitly

Explicitly send alerts practically via Slack or Email when issues occur
clearly:

◆ Slack Alert Example Explicitly:

```python

from slack_sdk import WebClient

import os

from dotenv import load_dotenv
```

```python
load_dotenv()
SLACK_BOT_TOKEN = os.getenv("SLACK_BOT_TOKEN")
client = WebClient(token=SLACK_BOT_TOKEN)


def send_alert_slack(message):
    client.chat_postMessage(channel="#alerts",
text=message)


send_alert_slack("Task failure explicitly detected
practically!")
```

◆ **Email Alert Example Explicitly:**

python

```python
import smtplib, ssl
from email.mime.text import MIMEText
from email.mime.multipart import MIMEMultipart


smtp_server = "smtp.gmail.com"
port = 465
sender_email = os.getenv("EMAIL_ADDRESS")
password = os.getenv("EMAIL_PASSWORD")


def send_email_alert(receiver_email, subject,
body):
    message = MIMEMultipart()
    message["From"] = sender_email
```

```python
    message["To"] = receiver_email

    message["Subject"] = subject

    message.attach(MIMEText(body, "plain"))


    context = ssl.create_default_context()

    with smtplib.SMTP_SSL(smtp_server, port,
context=context) as server:

        server.login(sender_email, password)

        server.sendmail(sender_email,
receiver_email, message.as_string())


send_email_alert("admin@example.com", "Workflow
Alert explicitly", "Task failure practically
detected explicitly.")
```

Best Practices Checklist Explicitly

Clear explicit practical checklist:

Implement detailed structured logging explicitly practically.

Collect explicit clear metrics practically (duration, success rates).

Trace workflow execution explicitly practically.

Set up explicit practical alerts clearly for critical issues.

Regularly review explicit logs practically for continuous improvement.

Common Issues and Explicit Solutions Practically

Clear practical troubleshooting explicitly:

Issue	Clear Practical Solution Explicitly
Missing Logs or Metrics	Verify logging configurations explicitly practically.
Excessive Alerting	Clearly configure practical alert thresholds explicitly.
Inaccurate Metrics	Validate explicit timing mechanisms practically clearly.

Security Considerations Explicitly

Explicitly avoid logging sensitive data practically.

Secure alerting channels explicitly practically (encrypted connections).

Practical Example: Comprehensive Monitoring Explicitly

A clear explicit workflow practically demonstrating full monitoring explicitly:

python

```python
import logging, time
from slack_sdk import WebClient
import os
from dotenv import load_dotenv

load_dotenv()
SLACK_BOT_TOKEN = os.getenv("SLACK_BOT_TOKEN")
client = WebClient(token=SLACK_BOT_TOKEN)
```

```python
logging.basicConfig(filename='comprehensive.log',
level=logging.INFO)


def monitored_task(task_name, task_func):

    logging.info(f"Task explicitly started
practically: {task_name}")

    start_time = time.time()

    try:

        task_func()

        logging.info(f"Task explicitly completed
practically: {task_name}")

    except Exception as e:

        logging.error(f"Task explicitly failed
practically: {task_name} with error {e}")

        client.chat_postMessage(channel="#alerts",
text=f"Failure explicitly: {task_name}")

    duration = time.time() - start_time

    logging.info(f"Task duration explicitly:
{duration} seconds practically")


monitored_task("Fetch Data explicitly", lambda:
time.sleep(1))
```

Practical Enhancements Explicitly

Implement explicit monitoring dashboards practically (e.g., Grafana,
Datadog).

Automated log analysis explicitly practically.

Summary & Next Steps

In this clear, practical section, you've explicitly learned:

- Monitoring and observability practically explicitly for autonomous workflows.
- Practical explicit implementation clearly demonstrated step-by-step.
- Best practices explicitly for effective workflow monitoring practically.

You're now explicitly prepared practically to implement comprehensive monitoring clearly, ensuring the reliability, transparency, and robustness of your autonomous workflows explicitly.

7.5 Project: Autonomous Marketing Automation Agent

In this practical, hands-on project, you'll build an **Autonomous Marketing Automation Agent** explicitly capable of automating marketing workflows practically, such as gathering leads, analyzing marketing data, personalizing email campaigns, and delivering automated performance reports clearly and explicitly.

Project Explicitly

Goal Practically:

- Build an autonomous marketing agent explicitly capable of:
- Fetching and analyzing real-time marketing data practically.
- Storing and managing lead information explicitly in databases.
- Automatically generating personalized email campaigns practically.
- Reporting campaign performance clearly via Slack or Email explicitly.

Real-world Relevance Explicitly:

This agent automates key marketing processes practically, enhancing efficiency explicitly and practically enabling data-driven decisions clearly.

Step-by-Step Project Guide Practically and Explicitly

Follow these clear explicit steps practically:

Step	Clearly Defined Stage	Practical Explanation Clearly
1	Set Up Project Environment explicitly	Explicitly install dependencies practically.
2	Fetch Marketing Data Explicitly via REST API	Clearly retrieve data practically.
3	Store and Manage Lead Data explicitly in SQLite	Implement practical explicit database clearly.
4	Autonomous Personalized Email Generation Explicitly	Practical explicit email personalization.
5	Send Campaign Reports Practically via Slack or Email	Deliver explicit practical insights clearly.

Step 1: Set Up Project Environment Explicitly

Create your environment practically:

bash

```
mkdir marketing-agent

cd marketing-agent

python -m venv env

source env/bin/activate    # macOS/Linux

.\env\Scripts\activate     # Windows


pip install requests sqlite3 openai slack_sdk
python-dotenv
```

Configure `.env` explicitly:

ini

```
OPENAI_API_KEY="your-openai-key"
SLACK_BOT_TOKEN="your-slack-token"
EMAIL_ADDRESS="your-email"
EMAIL_PASSWORD="your-email-password"
```

Step 2: Fetch Marketing Data Explicitly via REST API

Practical explicit example fetching marketing data:

python

```python
import requests

def fetch_marketing_data():
    url = "https://api.example.com/marketing/leads"
    response = requests.get(url)
    return response.json() if response.status_code == 200 else {}

leads_data = fetch_marketing_data()
print(leads_data)
```

Step 3: Store and Manage Lead Data Explicitly in SQLite

Explicitly manage lead data practically:

python

```python
import sqlite3

def create_leads_db():
    conn = sqlite3.connect('leads.db')
    cursor = conn.cursor()
    cursor.execute('''
        CREATE TABLE IF NOT EXISTS leads (
            id INTEGER PRIMARY KEY AUTOINCREMENT,
            name TEXT,
            email TEXT UNIQUE,
            source TEXT
        )
    ''')
    conn.commit()
    conn.close()

def store_leads(leads):
    conn = sqlite3.connect('leads.db')
    cursor = conn.cursor()
    for lead in leads:
        cursor.execute('INSERT OR IGNORE INTO leads (name, email, source) VALUES (?, ?, ?)',
                       (lead['name'], lead['email'], lead['source']))
    conn.commit()
```

```python
    conn.close()


create_leads_db()

store_leads(leads_data.get('leads', []))
```

Step 4: Autonomous Personalized Email Generation Explicitly

Generate practical personalized emails explicitly using OpenAI:

python

```python
import openai, sqlite3, os

from dotenv import load_dotenv


load_dotenv()

openai.api_key = os.getenv("OPENAI_API_KEY")


def generate_personalized_email(name):

    prompt = f"""

    You are an autonomous marketing assistant.

    Generate a short, personalized promotional
email explicitly to {name}.
    """


    response = openai.ChatCompletion.create(

        model="gpt-4-turbo",

        messages=[{"role": "system", "content":
prompt}],
```

```python
        temperature=0.3,

        max_tokens=150

    )

    return
response.choices[0].message.content.strip()


def prepare_emails():

    conn = sqlite3.connect('leads.db')

    cursor = conn.cursor()

    cursor.execute('SELECT name, email FROM leads')

    leads = cursor.fetchall()

    conn.close()


    emails = []

    for name, email in leads:

        content = generate_personalized_email(name)

        emails.append({"email": email, "content":
content})

    return emails


personalized_emails = prepare_emails()

print(personalized_emails)
```

Step 5: Send Campaign Reports Practically via Slack

Explicitly send reports practically using Slack:

python

```python
from slack_sdk import WebClient


SLACK_BOT_TOKEN = os.getenv("SLACK_BOT_TOKEN")
client = WebClient(token=SLACK_BOT_TOKEN)


def send_slack_report(message):
    client.chat_postMessage(channel="#marketing-reports", text=message)


send_slack_report("Marketing campaign emails explicitly generated practically!")
```

Alternative: Send Reports via Email Explicitly Practically

Explicitly send campaign updates practically via Email:

python

```python
import smtplib, ssl
from email.mime.text import MIMEText
from email.mime.multipart import MIMEMultipart


smtp_server = "smtp.gmail.com"
port = 465
sender_email = os.getenv("EMAIL_ADDRESS")
password = os.getenv("EMAIL_PASSWORD")
```

```python
def send_email_report(receiver_email, subject,
body):

    message = MIMEMultipart()

    message["From"] = sender_email

    message["To"] = receiver_email

    message["Subject"] = subject

    message.attach(MIMEText(body, "plain"))


    context = ssl.create_default_context()

    with smtplib.SMTP_SSL(smtp_server, port,
context=context) as server:

        server.login(sender_email, password)

        server.sendmail(sender_email,
receiver_email, message.as_string())


send_email_report("manager@example.com", "Campaign
Update explicitly", "Personalized emails generated
practically.")
```

Best Practices Checklist Explicitly

Clear explicit practical checklist:

Secure credentials explicitly practically.

Validate and store explicit lead data clearly.

Generate explicit personalized content practically.

Monitor explicit campaign metrics practically clearly.

Explicitly log practical workflow activities.

Common Issues and Explicit Solutions Practically

Clear practical troubleshooting explicitly:

Issue	Clear Practical Solution Explicitly
Email Delivery Issues	Explicitly verify SMTP credentials practically.
Data Integrity Errors	Explicitly handle duplicate leads practically clearly.
API Data Issues	Verify REST API endpoints explicitly practically.

Security Considerations Explicitly

Securely manage lead data explicitly practically.

Use secure channels explicitly practically for email communications clearly.

Practical Enhancements Explicitly

Automate explicit lead scoring practically.

Integrate campaign metrics explicitly practically with analytics platforms.

Summary & Next Steps

In this practical explicit project, you've clearly learned:

- Practically fetching, storing, and managing marketing data explicitly.
- Autonomous personalized email generation explicitly practically.
- Automated explicit reporting clearly and practically.

You're now explicitly equipped practically to build powerful marketing automation agents clearly, significantly enhancing marketing efficiency practically.

Chapter 8: Optimizing, Deploying, and Scaling Your Agents

Effectively **optimizing, deploying, and scaling** your autonomous agents explicitly ensures reliable, high-performing, and cost-effective real-world operations practically. This chapter practically guides you step-by-step explicitly through best practices and techniques clearly designed for enhancing performance, reliability, and scalability explicitly in real-world deployments practically.

Why Optimization, Deployment, and Scaling Matter Explicitly

Clear explicit practical benefits include:

- **Improved Performance:** Faster responses explicitly and practically optimized resource use.
- **High Reliability:** Minimized downtime explicitly and practical error management.
- **Cost Efficiency:** Explicitly reduced operational costs practically through optimized resource allocation.
- **Scalability:** Clearly handle increased workloads practically with minimal friction explicitly.

8.1 Optimization for Cost and Efficiency

Explicitly optimizing autonomous agents practically for **cost and efficiency** ensures maximum performance clearly while minimizing operational expenses explicitly. This section provides clear, practical, step-by-step strategies explicitly designed to help you practically improve agent responsiveness, reduce resource usage, and control costs effectively and explicitly.

Why Optimize for Cost and Efficiency Explicitly?

Clear explicit practical benefits include:

- **Cost Savings:** Practically reducing operational expenses explicitly.
- **Improved Performance:** Faster, more responsive agents explicitly.
- **Scalable Operations:** Efficiently handle increased workloads explicitly practically.

- **Resource Conservation:** Explicitly utilize resources practically optimally.

Key Areas for Cost and Efficiency Optimization Explicitly

Optimization Area	Explicit Practical Explanation
Prompt Efficiency	Clearly design efficient prompts explicitly practically.
API Management	Minimize explicit API calls practically clearly.
Compute Resources	Optimize CPU and memory usage explicitly practically.
Data Management	Efficient explicit storage and retrieval practically.

Practical Strategies for Optimization Explicitly

◆ **Efficient Prompt Engineering Explicitly**

Explicitly design practical concise prompts clearly:

```python
# Inefficient prompt explicitly:

prompt = "Explain clearly in detail all steps
practically to solve this issue."


# Efficient practical prompt explicitly:

prompt = "Clearly list practical key steps
explicitly."
```

◆ **Reducing API Calls Practically Explicitly**

Batch API calls clearly practically to reduce explicit requests:

```python
python

# Multiple individual requests explicitly
(inefficient)
for id in item_ids:
    fetch_data(id)


# Efficient batching explicitly practically
fetch_batch_data(item_ids)
```

◆ Resource Allocation Explicitly Practically

Clearly optimize explicit resource allocation practically using resource monitoring:

Explicitly monitor memory and CPU usage practically.

Scale explicit resources practically based on real-time needs clearly.

Practical Tools Explicitly:

`htop`, Docker stats, AWS CloudWatch

◆ Efficient Data Storage Practically Explicitly

Clear explicit practical example using indexing:

```sql
sql

-- Inefficient explicit query practically (slow)
SELECT * FROM users WHERE email='user@example.com';
```

```
-- Efficient indexed explicit query practically
(fast)

CREATE INDEX idx_email ON users (email);
```

Example: Cost-Effective API Usage Explicitly Practically

Explicitly practical example clearly reducing API calls explicitly:

python

```python
def batch_request(ids):
    batched_ids = ','.join(ids)
    response =
requests.get(f"https://api.example.com/data?ids={ba
tched_ids}")
    return response.json()


data = batch_request(['id1', 'id2', 'id3'])
```

Monitoring for Efficiency Practically Explicitly

Clearly practical explicit logging explicitly:

python

```python
import logging, time


logging.basicConfig(filename='efficiency.log',
level=logging.INFO)


start_time = time.time()
```

```
# Explicit practical task

end_time = time.time()


logging.info(f"Task duration explicitly
practically: {end_time - start_time}s")
```

Cost Management in Cloud Deployments Explicitly Practically

Explicitly utilize spot instances practically for cost savings.

Implement explicit practical auto-scaling clearly based on real-time metrics.

Example Explicitly Practically (AWS):

- AWS EC2 Spot Instances explicitly.
- AWS Auto Scaling Groups practically.

Best Practices Checklist Explicitly

Clear explicit practical checklist:

- Optimize prompts explicitly practically.
- Batch API requests explicitly practically.
- Explicitly monitor resource usage clearly practically.
- Efficiently store and retrieve data explicitly practically.
- Regularly review explicit practical logs for inefficiencies.

Common Issues and Explicit Solutions Practically

Clear practical troubleshooting explicitly:

Issue	Clear Practical Solution Explicitly
High API Costs	Batch explicit API requests practically clearly.
Slow Performance	Optimize explicit prompts practically clearly.

227

Issue	Clear Practical Solution Explicitly
Resource Waste	Monitor explicitly practically resource allocation clearly.

Security Considerations Explicitly

- Explicitly secure practical API credentials clearly.
- Clearly manage explicit access practically to optimize security explicitly.

Practical Project Example: Optimized Autonomous Agent Explicitly

Implement explicit practical efficiency improvements clearly:

python

```
import requests, logging


logging.basicConfig(filename='optimized_agent.log',
level=logging.INFO)


def efficient_fetch(ids):
    batched_ids = ','.join(ids)
    response =
requests.get(f"https://api.example.com/data?ids={ba
tched_ids}")
    logging.info(f"API called explicitly
practically for {len(ids)} items")
    return response.json()


data = efficient_fetch(['item1', 'item2', 'item3'])
```

```
print(data)
```

Practical Enhancements Explicitly

- Implement explicit cost-tracking dashboards practically.
- Utilize explicit practical predictive scaling clearly.

Summary & Next Steps

In this clear, practical section, you've explicitly learned:

- Optimizing explicit practical agents for cost-efficiency clearly.
- Explicit practical strategies clearly demonstrated step-by-step.
- Monitoring explicit agent performance practically for continucus improvement.

You're now explicitly prepared practically to optimize autonomous agents clearly, ensuring cost-effective, efficient, and reliable real-world operations explicitly practically.

8.3 Deployment Options (Docker, Kubernetes, Cloud Platforms)

Deploying your autonomous agents effectively ensures they are robust, reliable, and easily manageable in real-world environments. This section guides you step-by-step through popular deployment strategies using **Docker**, **Kubernetes**, and various **cloud platforms**, enabling efficient and scalable operations.

Why Choosing the Right Deployment Option Matters

Deployment decisions directly affect:

- **Scalability**: Quickly adjusting resources to meet demand.
- **Reliability**: Ensuring agents run consistently with minimal downtime.
- **Manageability**: Easily updating, monitoring, and maintaining agents.
- **Cost Efficiency**: Optimizing expenses through smart resource allocation.

Key Deployment Options and Practical Uses

Deployment Method	Practical Use Cases
Docker	Containerized applications; local, lightweight deployments
Kubernetes	Scalable container orchestration for robust workloads
Cloud Platforms	Managed services for seamless deployment at scale (AWS, GCP, Azure)

Docker Deployment: Step-by-Step Practical Guide

Docker simplifies agent deployment by packaging your agents and their dependencies into portable, reusable containers.

Step 1: Create a Dockerfile

Clearly define your Dockerfile:

```dockerfile
FROM python:3.11-slim

WORKDIR /app

COPY requirements.txt .

RUN pip install --no-cache-dir -r requirements.txt

COPY . .
```

```
CMD ["python", "agent_main.py"]
```

Step 2: Build Your Docker Image

Execute clearly from your project's root folder:

```bash
docker build -t autonomous-agent:latest .
```

Step 3: Run Your Docker Container

Practically run your agent with:

```bash
docker run -d --name agent-container autonomous-agent:latest
```

Common Docker Commands

Command	Purpose
`docker ps`	List running containers
`docker logs agent-container`	Check logs of your container
`docker stop agent-container`	Stop your container
`docker rm agent-container`	Remove stopped container

Kubernetes Deployment: Step-by-Step Practical Guide

Kubernetes efficiently orchestrates multiple agent containers, enabling high scalability and reliability.

Step 1: Containerize your Application with Docker (As Above)

Ensure you have a built Docker image pushed to a registry (Docker Hub, AWS ECR, GCP Container Registry).

Step 2: Create Kubernetes Deployment YAML File

Example clearly provided (agent-deployment.yaml):

yaml

```yaml
apiVersion: apps/v1
kind: Deployment
metadata:
  name: agent-deployment
spec:
  replicas: 3
  selector:
    matchLabels:
      app: autonomous-agent
  template:
    metadata:
      labels:
        app: autonomous-agent
    spec:
      containers:
      - name: autonomous-agent
        image: your-docker-image-url:latest
        ports:
        - containerPort: 8000
```

Step 3: Deploy Your Application to Kubernetes

Apply practically using kubectl:

bash

```
kubectl apply -f agent-deployment.yaml
```

Step 4: Check Deployment Status

Ensure agents are running clearly:

```
bash
```

```
kubectl get deployments
```

```
kubectl get pods
```

Kubernetes Best Practices

- Use namespaces clearly for isolation.
- Define resource requests and limits practically.
- Use health checks explicitly (`readinessProbe`, `livenessProbe`).

Deploying on Cloud Platforms: AWS, GCP, Azure

Cloud platforms provide managed services making deployment straightforward and efficient.

AWS: ECS (Elastic Container Service) Practical Guide

- Push Docker images explicitly to Amazon ECR.
- Create an ECS Cluster practically.
- Define task definitions explicitly pointing to your ECR image.
- Launch services practically and set up auto-scaling.

Example: Task definition in JSON explicitly:

```
json
```

```
{
  "family": "autonomous-agent",
  "networkMode": "awsvpc",
  "containerDefinitions": [
```

```json
{
    "name": "agent",
    "image":
"123456789012.dkr.ecr.region.amazonaws.com/agent:la
test",
    "portMappings": [{"containerPort": 8000,
"hostPort": 8000}],
    "memory": 512,
    "cpu": 256
  }
],
"requiresCompatibilities": ["FARGATE"],
"cpu": "256",
"memory": "512"
}
```

Google Cloud Platform: Cloud Run Practical Guide

Cloud Run simplifies deployment using container images:

Build your Docker image practically and push to GCP Container Registry.

Deploy explicitly to Cloud Run:

bash

```bash
gcloud run deploy autonomous-agent \
  --image gcr.io/your-project/agent:latest \
  --platform managed \
  --region us-central1 \
  --allow-unauthenticated
```

Azure: Azure Container Instances Practical Guide

Deploy agents practically on Azure using containers:

bash

```
az container create \
  --resource-group YourResourceGroup \
  --name autonomous-agent \
  --image yourregistry.azurecr.io/agent:latest \
  --cpu 1 \
  --memory 1.5 \
  --ports 8000 \
  --dns-name-label agent-demo \
  --location eastus
```

Best Practices for Production Deployment

Follow these best practices explicitly for production-quality deployments:

- Automate deployments practically using CI/CD pipelines (GitHub Actions, GitLab CI/CD).
- Implement versioning explicitly and rollbacks.
- Regularly monitor practically and review logs for anomalies.
- Securely manage environment variables and secrets explicitly (AWS Secrets Manager, Azure Key Vault).

Common Issues and Clear Solutions

Issue	Clear Practical Solution
Docker build failures	Verify Dockerfile syntax and dependencies explicitly
Kubernetes pod issues	Check pod logs using `kubectl logs <pod-name>`
Cloud deployment errors	Confirm permissions and resource configurations explicitly

Security Considerations

- Regularly update container images explicitly.
- Use private container registries practically.
- Implement explicit resource access policies.

Practical Project Example: Autonomous Agent CI/CD Pipeline

Set up a practical, explicit Continuous Deployment pipeline clearly using GitHub Actions:

GitHub Action YAML (`deploy-agent.yaml`):

```yaml
name: Deploy Autonomous Agent

on:
  push:
    branches:
      - main
```

```yaml
jobs:
  build-and-push:
    runs-on: ubuntu-latest
    steps:
      - uses: actions/checkout@v4

      - name: Login to Docker Hub
        uses: docker/login-action@v3
        with:
          username: ${{ secrets.DOCKER_USERNAME }}
          password: ${{ secrets.DOCKER_PASSWORD }}

      - name: Build and Push Docker image
        uses: docker/build-push-action@v5
        with:
          context: .
          push: true
          tags: yourdockerhubusername/autonomous-agent:latest

  deploy:
    runs-on: ubuntu-latest
    needs: build-and-push
    steps:
      - uses: actions/checkout@v4
```

```
    - name: Deploy to Cloud Run

      uses: google-github-actions/deploy-
cloudrun@v2

      with:

        service: autonomous-agent

        image:
docker.io/yourdockerhubusername/autonomous-
agent:latest

        region: us-central1

        credentials: ${{ secrets.GCP_CREDENTIALS
}}
```

Practical Enhancements

Implement monitoring explicitly with services like Prometheus or Datadog.

Configure auto-scaling practically for handling traffic spikes efficiently.

Summary & Next Steps

In this section, you've learned practical steps for deploying your autonomous agents clearly using Docker, Kubernetes, and cloud platforms. You've explored best practices explicitly to ensure reliable and scalable agent deployment practically.

8.4 Best Practices for Scaling Autonomous Agents

Effectively **scaling autonomous agents** ensures they can handle increased workloads, maintain performance, and operate reliably in real-world scenarios. This section provides practical, step-by-step guidance on best practices for scaling your agents efficiently, reliably, and cost-effectively.

Importance of Proper Scaling

Proper scaling ensures:

- **Reliability**: Agents consistently meet user demand.

- **Performance**: Fast responses under varying workloads.
- **Cost-effectiveness**: Optimal resource use, avoiding unnecessary expenses.
- **Flexibility**: Ability to quickly adapt to changing traffic patterns.

Key Concepts in Scaling Autonomous Agents

Two primary approaches clearly defined:

- **Horizontal Scaling**: Increasing the number of agent instances.
- **Vertical Scaling**: Adding resources (CPU, RAM) to existing agents.

Scaling Approach Practical Use Cases

Horizontal	Handling variable or high traffic explicitly
Vertical	Optimizing performance for resource-intensive tasks

Practical Best Practices for Scaling Autonomous Agents

Follow these best practices explicitly for robust, scalable agents:

1. Containerization (Docker) and Orchestration (Kubernetes)

Clearly containerize agents to simplify deployment and scaling.

Use **Docker** explicitly for consistent, repeatable environments.

Deploy practically on **Kubernetes** for efficient orchestration and automated scaling.

Kubernetes Example for Horizontal Scaling:

yaml

```
apiVersion: autoscaling/v1

kind: HorizontalPodAutoscaler

metadata:

  name: agent-autoscaler
```

```
spec:

  scaleTargetRef:

    apiVersion: apps/v1

    kind: Deployment

    name: autonomous-agent

  minReplicas: 2

  maxReplicas: 10

  targetCPUUtilizationPercentage: 70
```

2. Auto-Scaling Explicitly Based on Metrics

Automatically scale practically using metrics such as:

CPU usage explicitly.

Memory utilization practically.

Network traffic explicitly.

Custom metrics (e.g., task queues, requests).

Example: AWS ECS Autoscaling based on CPU:

Clearly define ECS Autoscaling policies explicitly.

Trigger practically when CPU exceeds threshold:

```
mathematica
```

```
Scale out: CPU > 70% for 5 minutes → Add instances
Scale in: CPU < 30% for 10 minutes → Remove
instances
```

3. Efficient Resource Allocation

Optimize resources explicitly for practical cost-efficiency:

Regularly monitor explicitly using tools such as CloudWatch, Datadog, or Grafana.

Set explicit resource limits practically to prevent overspending.

Practical Kubernetes resource limits:

yaml

```
resources:
  requests:
    memory: "512Mi"
    cpu: "250m"
  limits:
    memory: "1Gi"
    cpu: "500m"
```

4. Load Balancing and Traffic Management

Ensure requests are clearly distributed efficiently across agent instances practically.

Use explicit load balancers (AWS ELB, GCP Cloud Load Balancer).

Implement clear strategies practically like Round-Robin or Least Connections.

5. Stateless Agent Design

Explicitly design agents as stateless practically for easier scaling:

Store agent state explicitly externally (Redis, PostgreSQL, MongoDB).

Avoid relying explicitly on local state practically.

6. Caching and Content Delivery Networks (CDNs)

Practically reduce explicit agent workload by caching frequent responses explicitly:

Use Redis or Memcached explicitly for caching practical responses.

Integrate practically with CDNs explicitly (Cloudflare, AWS CloudFront) to reduce load.

---

7. Continuous Monitoring and Alerting

Constantly monitor practically your agent's health and performance explicitly:

Use Prometheus explicitly with Grafana practically for real-time metrics.

Set up clear alerts practically for performance degradation explicitly.

Example Prometheus Alert Rule:

yaml

```
groups:
  - name: agent_performance_alerts
    rules:
      - alert: HighAgentCPUUsage
        expr:
avg(rate(container_cpu_usage_seconds_total{pod=~"ag
ent.*"}[5m])) > 0.75
        for: 5m
        labels:
          severity: critical
        annotations:
          summary: "High CPU usage detected on
agents"
```

Common Issues and Practical Solutions

Issue	Clear Practical Solution
Uneven load distribution	Configure load balancer algorithms explicitly
Resource contention	Implement resource limits practically
Slow scaling reaction	Adjust autoscaling thresholds explicitly
State management problems	Ensure agents are stateless practically

Security Considerations for Scaling

Secure explicit scaling APIs practically.

Monitor practically for abnormal scaling events explicitly.

Regularly audit clear scaling policies and configurations practically.

Best Practices Checklist for Scaling Agents

Follow this practical checklist explicitly:

- Containerize and orchestrate explicitly.
- Implement clear autoscaling practically.
- Monitor explicit metrics clearly.
- Use efficient load balancing explicitly.
- Maintain stateless design practically.
- Cache frequently accessed data explicitly.

Practical Project Example: Scalable Autonomous Agent Setup

Implement a practical, explicit example of scalable autonomous agents using Docker, Kubernetes, and autoscaling:

Step 1: Containerize Agent with Docker

Create a `Dockerfile` explicitly (as shown previously).

Build and push clearly:

```bash
bash
```

```bash
docker build -t yourrepo/autonomous-agent:latest .
docker push yourrepo/autonomous-agent:latest
```

Step 2: Deploy to Kubernetes Practically

`agent-deployment.yaml` explicitly defined:

```yaml
yaml
```

```yaml
apiVersion: apps/v1
kind: Deployment
metadata:
  name: autonomous-agent
spec:
  replicas: 2
  selector:
    matchLabels:
      app: autonomous-agent
  template:
    metadata:
      labels:
        app: autonomous-agent
    spec:
      containers:
      - name: agent
        image: yourrepo/autonomous-agent:latest
```

```
      resources:
        requests:
          memory: "512Mi"
          cpu: "250m"
        limits:
          memory: "1Gi"
          cpu: "500m"
```

Deploy explicitly:

bash

```
kubectl apply -f agent-deployment.yaml
```

Step 3: Setup Autoscaling Practically

agent-autoscaler.yaml clearly defined:

yaml

```
apiVersion: autoscaling/v1
kind: HorizontalPodAutoscaler
metadata:
  name: autonomous-agent-hpa
spec:
  scaleTargetRef:
    apiVersion: apps/v1
    kind: Deployment
    name: autonomous-agent
  minReplicas: 2
  maxReplicas: 10
```

```
targetCPUUtilizationPercentage: 70
```

Apply explicitly:

```
bash
```

```
kubectl apply -f agent-autoscaler.yaml
```

Practical Enhancements

Implement explicit predictive scaling practically.

Set up explicit advanced monitoring dashboards (e.g., Grafana).

Summary & Next Steps

In this section, you've learned practical, explicit best practices for scaling autonomous agents, including horizontal and vertical scaling, efficient resource allocation, and proactive monitoring. You're now equipped to build reliable, scalable, and cost-effective autonomous agents ready for real-world deployment.

8.5 Maintaining Your Agents in Production

Once your autonomous agents are deployed, maintaining them effectively ensures reliability, consistent performance, and robust operations over the long term. This section provides clear, step-by-step practical guidance on best practices for production maintenance, including monitoring, updates, troubleshooting, and ongoing optimization.

Importance of Maintenance in Production

Regular maintenance helps ensure:

Reliability: Agents operate consistently without unexpected downtime.

Security: Protecting agents and data from vulnerabilities.

Performance: Maintaining optimal speed and resource utilization.

Adaptability: Swiftly responding to changing conditions and requirements.

Key Components of Production Maintenance

Practically maintaining autonomous agents involves clear management of:

Component	Practical Explanation
Monitoring	Tracking agent health and performance
Logging	Recording events and errors for troubleshooting
Updates & Patches	Regular software updates and security patches
Backup & Recovery	Safeguarding data and ensuring continuity
Incident Response	Promptly handling and resolving production incidents

Practical Steps for Effective Maintenance

1. Continuous Monitoring

Proactively monitor agent performance and health using practical tools:

Prometheus/Grafana for real-time metrics visualization.

AWS CloudWatch or **Azure Monitor** for cloud deployments.

Example Prometheus Configuration:

yaml

```
scrape_configs:
  - job_name: 'agent-monitoring'
    static_configs:
      - targets: ['agent-service:8000']
```

2. Comprehensive Logging Strategy

Implement detailed logging practically for easier troubleshooting:

Use structured logging explicitly.

Rotate logs clearly to prevent storage overload.

Python Logging Configuration Example:

python

```
import logging
from logging.handlers import RotatingFileHandler


logger = logging.getLogger('agentLogger')
logger.setLevel(logging.INFO)


handler = RotatingFileHandler('agent.log',
maxBytes=10485760, backupCount=5)
formatter = logging.Formatter('%(asctime)s
%(levelname)s %(message)s')
handler.setFormatter(formatter)


logger.addHandler(handler)
logger.info("Agent started successfully.")
```

---

3. Regular Updates and Security Patching

Ensure agents and dependencies are always up-to-date to avoid vulnerabilities:

Automate updates using CI/CD pipelines practically.

Regularly check for security advisories explicitly.

Practical Example: Scheduled Dependency Updates (GitHub Actions):

```yaml
yaml

name: Dependency Update

on:
  schedule:
    - cron: '0 0 * * 0'  # every Sunday at midnight

jobs:
  update-dependencies:
    runs-on: ubuntu-latest
    steps:
      - uses: actions/checkout@v4

      - name: Update Dependencies
        run: |
          pip install --upgrade pip
          pip install pip-tools
          pip-compile --upgrade requirements.in

      - name: Create Pull Request
        uses: peter-evans/create-pull-request@v6
        with:
          title: "Automated Dependency Updates"
          branch: dependency-updates
```

4. Backup and Disaster Recovery Planning

Regularly back up critical data explicitly and practically test recovery procedures:

Backup databases explicitly (PostgreSQL, MongoDB).

Use cloud storage practically for backups (AWS S3, Google Cloud Storage).

Example: Backup SQLite database explicitly:

bash

```
sqlite3 agent.db ".backup agent-backup-$(date
+%F).db"

aws s3 cp agent-backup-$(date +%F).db s3://my-
agent-backups/
```

5. Incident Response and Troubleshooting

Develop clear, practical incident response plans explicitly:

Define roles clearly and escalation paths explicitly.

Set up practical alerting systems clearly (Slack, PagerDuty, email).

Example: Incident Notification via Slack:

python

```
from slack_sdk import WebClient
import os
from dotenv import load_dotenv

load_dotenv()
client =
WebClient(token=os.getenv("SLACK_BOT_TOKEN"))
```

```
def notify_incident(message):

    client.chat_postMessage(channel="#incidents",
text=message)


notify_incident("Critical: Agent downtime
detected.")
```

Best Practices Checklist for Production Maintenance

Follow these clear, practical guidelines explicitly:

- Implement continuous monitoring practically.
- Maintain structured and rotated logs explicitly.
- Regularly apply updates and security patches clearly.
- Schedule frequent backups practically.
- Establish and regularly test an explicit incident response plan.

Common Issues and Practical Solutions

Issue	Clear Practical Solution
Unexpected downtime	Improve monitoring explicitly and practical alerting
Performance degradation	Analyze logs and metrics clearly to optimize tasks
Security vulnerabilities	Regularly update dependencies and apply patches explicitly
Data loss	Implement regular backups and recovery tests practically

Security Considerations for Maintenance

Regularly audit access explicitly to production environments.

Rotate credentials practically and manage them securely (AWS Secrets Manager, Azure Key Vault).

Practical Project Example: Automated Maintenance Pipeline

Set up practical automated maintenance explicitly with GitHub Actions:

Maintenance Pipeline (`maintenance.yml`):

yaml

```
name: Production Maintenance

on:
  schedule:
    - cron: '0 3 * * *'  # daily at 3 AM

jobs:
  backups:
    runs-on: ubuntu-latest
    steps:
      - uses: actions/checkout@v4

      - name: Backup Database and Upload to AWS S3
        env:
          AWS_ACCESS_KEY_ID: ${{
secrets.AWS_ACCESS_KEY_ID }}
          AWS_SECRET_ACCESS_KEY: ${{
secrets.AWS_SECRET_ACCESS_KEY }}
        run: |
```

```
        sqlite3 agent.db ".backup agent-backup-
$(date +%F).db"

        aws s3 cp agent-backup-$(date +%F).db
s3://agent-production-backups/


  security-updates:

    runs-on: ubuntu-latest

    steps:

      - uses: actions/checkout@v4


      - name: Check for Security Vulnerabilities

        run: |

          pip install safety

          safety check --file=requirements.txt --
full-report
```

Practical Enhancements for Maintenance

Integrate explicit AI-driven monitoring practically (e.g., Datadog APM).

Conduct explicit chaos engineering tests practically to ensure resilience.

Summary & Next Steps

In this section, you've learned practical, explicit methods to effectively maintain your autonomous agents in production, including proactive monitoring, structured logging, regular updates, and robust incident response. You're now equipped to confidently ensure the reliability, security, and high performance of your agents long-term.

Chapter 9. Security, Ethics, and Regulatory Compliance

When developing, deploying, and managing autonomous agents powered by AI, maintaining high standards for **security, ethical responsibility, and regulatory compliance** is critical. This chapter provides practical, step-by-step guidance on ensuring your agents operate securely, ethically, and within regulatory boundaries.

Importance of Security, Ethics, and Compliance

Properly addressing these areas ensures:

Trust: Users and stakeholders have confidence in your agents.

Safety: Minimizing potential harm from security breaches.

Legal Protection: Avoiding penalties by complying with regulations.

Reputation: Upholding strong ethical standards to protect your brand.

9.1 Ensuring Agent Security

Securing autonomous agents is critical to protecting sensitive data, maintaining user trust, and preventing unauthorized access or misuse. This section provides step-by-step practical guidance on how to implement robust security measures to ensure your agents operate safely and securely.

Importance of Agent Security

Strong security helps you:

Protect user and business data from breaches.

Prevent unauthorized access and misuse.

Comply with industry regulations.

Maintain trust and confidence from users and stakeholders.

Key Security Components for Autonomous Agents

To effectively secure your agents, clearly focus on these key areas:

Security Component	Practical Explanation
Authentication	Verifying the identity of users and agents
Authorization	Defining and managing permissions explicitly
Secure API Usage	Safeguarding API keys and endpoints practically
Data Encryption	Protecting data at rest and in transit explicitly
Logging & Monitoring	Quickly identifying and responding to threats

Step-by-Step Practical Guide to Agent Security

1. Authentication and Authorization

Use robust authentication methods explicitly (OAuth, JWT):

Practical Example: JWT Authentication

python

```python
import jwt
import datetime
import os

SECRET_KEY = os.getenv("JWT_SECRET_KEY")

def generate_token(user_id):
    payload = {
        'user_id': user_id,
        'exp': datetime.datetime.utcnow() +
datetime.timedelta(hours=1)
    }
```

```python
    token = jwt.encode(payload, SECRET_KEY,
algorithm='HS256')

    return token
```

```python
def verify_token(token):
    try:
        return jwt.decode(token, SECRET_KEY,
algorithms=['HS256'])

    except jwt.ExpiredSignatureError:

        return None
```

Explicit Authorization Example:

Use role-based access control practically:

python

```python
user_roles = {'user123': 'admin', 'user456':
'user'}


def is_authorized(user_id, required_role):
    return user_roles.get(user_id) == required_role
```

---

2. Secure API Key and Credential Management

Avoid hardcoding API keys; use environment variables practically:

Explicit Practical Example:

python

```python
import os

from dotenv import load_dotenv
```

```python
load_dotenv()

api_key = os.getenv('OPENAI_API_KEY')
```

Enhanced Security:
Use managed secret services explicitly:

AWS Secrets Manager

Azure Key Vault

HashiCorp Vault

---

3. Data Encryption (At Rest and In Transit)

Encrypt sensitive data clearly and explicitly:

Data Encryption at Rest (SQLite example):

python

```python
from cryptography.fernet import Fernet


key = Fernet.generate_key()
cipher_suite = Fernet(key)


def encrypt_data(data):
    return cipher_suite.encrypt(data.encode())


def decrypt_data(encrypted_data):
    return
cipher_suite.decrypt(encrypted_data).decode()
```

```
encrypted = encrypt_data("Sensitive User Data")
```

```
print(decrypt_data(encrypted))
```

Data Encryption in Transit (HTTPS):
Always use HTTPS explicitly to encrypt API communication.

---

4. Logging and Security Monitoring

Implement structured logging clearly for security monitoring:

Structured Logging Example:

python

```python
import logging

logging.basicConfig(
    filename='agent-security.log',
    level=logging.WARNING,
    format='%(asctime)s %(levelname)s %(message)s'
)


def log_unauthorized_access(user_id):
    logging.warning(f'Unauthorized access attempt
by user {user_id}')


log_unauthorized_access('user789')
```

---

5. Regular Security Audits and Testing

Conduct regular security audits practically:

Perform penetration tests explicitly.

Regularly scan dependencies for vulnerabilities practically.

Automated Security Scans (Safety for Python):

bash

```
pip install safety
safety check --file=requirements.txt
```

Security Best Practices Checklist

Follow this practical checklist explicitly:

- Implement secure authentication explicitly.
- Protect and manage API keys clearly.
- Encrypt sensitive data practically (at rest and in transit).
- Monitor and log suspicious activities explicitly.
- Regularly audit and test security explicitly.

Common Security Issues and Solutions

Issue	Practical Solution
Leaked API Keys	Use environment variables or secret managers explicitly
Unauthorized Access	Enforce strong authentication and authorization practically
Data Exposure	Encrypt data explicitly at rest and in transit practically
Unmonitored threats	Regularly monitor logs explicitly for suspicious activities

Security Considerations for Autonomous Agents

Regularly update dependencies explicitly.

Clearly define minimal necessary permissions practically (Principle of Least Privilege).

Implement explicit incident response strategies practically.

Practical Project Example: Secure Autonomous Agent Setup

Implement a practical, secure autonomous agent explicitly:

Step 1: Secure Credential Management (AWS Secrets Manager example)

python

```python
import boto3
import os
from dotenv import load_dotenv


load_dotenv()
secret_name = "OpenAI/APIKey"
region_name = "us-west-2"


def get_secret():
    session = boto3.session.Session()
    client = session.client('secretsmanager',
region_name=region_name)
    secret_value =
client.get_secret_value(SecretId=secret_name)
    return secret_value['SecretString']
```

```python
api_key = get_secret()
```

Step 2: Secure Communication with APIs (HTTPS)

python

```python
import requests

response = requests.get('https://secure-
api.openai.com/data', headers={'Authorization':
f'Bearer {api_key}'})
```

Step 3: Data Encryption at Rest

python

```python
from cryptography.fernet import Fernet

key = os.getenv("DATA_ENCRYPTION_KEY")
cipher_suite = Fernet(key)

def store_encrypted_data(data):
    encrypted_data =
cipher_suite.encrypt(data.encode())
    with open('secure_data.dat', 'wb') as file:
        file.write(encrypted_data)

def load_encrypted_data():
    with open('secure_data.dat', 'rb') as file:
        encrypted_data = file.read()
```

```
    return
cipher_suite.decrypt(encrypted_data).decode()


store_encrypted_data("Sensitive Agent Data")

print(load_encrypted_data())
```

Practical Security Enhancements

Integrate explicit AI-powered threat detection practically (e.g., AWS GuardDuty, Azure Security Center).

Implement explicit anomaly detection systems practically.

Summary & Next Steps

In this section, you've learned explicit, practical steps to secure your autonomous agents thoroughly—from secure authentication and encryption to effective logging and monitoring. You're now well-equipped practically to confidently implement robust security measures explicitly, ensuring your autonomous agents are safe and reliable.

9.2 Managing Sensitive Information

Handling **sensitive information** correctly is one of the most critical aspects of developing and deploying autonomous agents. Whether your agent processes user data, API credentials, or proprietary business information, improper handling can lead to data leaks, privacy violations, and non-compliance with regulations.

This section walks you through **best practices**, practical code examples, and tools to securely manage sensitive information in real-world production environments.

What Is Considered Sensitive Information?

Sensitive data includes:

Type	Examples
User Data	Names, emails, phone numbers, passwords, health data
Authentication Info	API keys, tokens, database credentials
Business Intelligence	Sales reports, internal KPIs, strategic plans
Model Outputs	AI-generated content that could reveal private info

Practical Principles for Handling Sensitive Information

Principle	What It Means Practically
Don't hardcode secrets	Never write secrets in code or version control
Use environment variables	Load credentials at runtime from a secure environment
Encrypt data	At rest and in transit using secure algorithms
Restrict access	Follow least-privilege access for data and credentials
Audit and rotate secrets	Regularly rotate keys and monitor for misuse

1. Avoid Hardcoding Credentials (Use `.env` Files)

Never do this:

```python
python
```

```python
api_key = "sk-123456789abcdef"  # Hardcoded API key
```

Use this instead:

```bash
bash
```

263

```
# .env file

OPENAI_API_KEY=sk-abc123xyz456

python
```

```python
from dotenv import load_dotenv
import os


load_dotenv()
api_key = os.getenv("OPENAI_API_KEY")
```

Make sure to add `.env` to your `.gitignore`:

```
bash
```

```
# .gitignore
.env
```

---

2. Use Secret Management Services in Production

For production-grade deployments, use secure secret managers:

Platform	Secret Manager
AWS	AWS Secrets Manager, AWS Parameter Store
Azure	Azure Key Vault
Google Cloud	Secret Manager
Docker/K8s	Docker Secrets, Kubernetes Secrets

Example: Fetching a secret from AWS Secrets Manager

```
python
```

```python
import boto3


def get_secret(secret_name, region_name='us-east-
1'):
    client = boto3.client('secretsmanager',
region_name=region_name)
    secret =
client.get_secret_value(SecretId=secret_name)
    return secret['SecretString']


api_key = get_secret("OpenAI/APIKey")
```

---

3. Encrypt Sensitive Data at Rest and in Transit

Encrypting data at rest (Python example using `cryptography`)

python

```python
from cryptography.fernet import Fernet


key = Fernet.generate_key()  # Store this securely!
cipher = Fernet(key)


# Encrypt and store
with open("data.txt", "wb") as f:
    f.write(cipher.encrypt(b"My sensitive info"))


# Read and decrypt
```

```python
with open("data.txt", "rb") as f:
    encrypted = f.read()
    print(cipher.decrypt(encrypted).decode())
```

Encrypting data in transit

Always use HTTPS for all external communications:

python

```python
import requests


response = requests.get("https://secure-api.com",
headers={"Authorization": f"Bearer {api_key}"})
```

---

4. Minimize Data Retention

Don't store sensitive information longer than necessary. If you must store it,
log as little as possible and set up automatic deletion policies.

Example: Deleting user data (SQLite)

python

```python
import sqlite3


def delete_user_data(user_id):
    conn = sqlite3.connect('users.db')
    cursor = conn.cursor()
    cursor.execute("DELETE FROM users WHERE id =
?", (user_id,))
    conn.commit()
    conn.close()
```

5. Mask Sensitive Output from Logs

Never log full API keys, passwords, or user PII.

Safe logging pattern:

```python

import logging


user_email = "jane@example.com"

logging.info(f"Processing data for user: {user_email[:3]}***@example.com")  # Masked email
```

6. Rotate Secrets Regularly

Set up schedules or use managed tools to rotate tokens and passwords periodically to prevent misuse.

Best tools for rotation:

AWS Secrets Manager (automatic rotation)

HashiCorp Vault (versioned secrets)

CI/CD secrets rotation pipelines (GitHub Actions, GitLab CI)

Best Practices Checklist

- Store credentials in environment variables or secret managers
- Use HTTPS for all API communication
- Encrypt sensitive data at rest
- Never commit secrets to version control
- Mask all sensitive values in logs
- Periodically rotate and audit credentials

Common Pitfalls and Fixes

Mistake	Fix It Like This
Hardcoded API keys	Load them via `.env` or cloud secret manager
Logging user passwords or emails	Mask PII before logging
Sending data over HTTP	Always use HTTPS
Storing too much sensitive info	Store only what's necessary and delete regularly

Summary

In this section, you learned how to properly handle sensitive information inside autonomous agents—from securely storing API keys to encrypting and minimizing data exposure. By applying these techniques, you reduce risk, improve compliance, and build safer AI-driven systems.

9.3 Ethical Considerations for Autonomous Agents

Autonomous agents make decisions, generate content, and take actions—often without direct human oversight. As a result, **ethical responsibility** is not optional; it's essential. This section outlines real-world, actionable practices to ensure your agents behave fairly, transparently, and responsibly.

Why Ethical Design Matters

Unethical behavior from AI systems can lead to:

- **Misinformation** or biased outputs
- **Discrimination** against users or groups
- **Loss of trust** from customers and stakeholders
- **Regulatory penalties** and legal exposure

Embedding ethical thinking into your development process reduces these risks and builds more inclusive, responsible, and trustworthy systems.

Core Ethical Principles for Autonomous Agents

Principle	Practical Meaning
Transparency	Make it clear when an agent is acting or making decisions
Fairness	Avoid biased outputs that discriminate against individuals or groups
Accountability	Ensure traceability of decisions and actions taken by the agent
Privacy	Respect user data and protect sensitive information
Human Oversight	Allow human intervention when necessary

1. Transparency in Agent Behavior

Users should always know when they're interacting with an AI system and what the system is doing.

Example: Inform Users Clearly

```text


Note: You are interacting with an autonomous agent.
Some responses are AI-generated based on previous
inputs and may not reflect human opinions.
```

Include explanations in logs and output messages when decisions are made automatically.

2. Bias Detection and Mitigation

Bias in training data or model outputs can lead to unfair or harmful results. Mitigate it using:

- Diverse training data
- Prompt tuning
- Output filtering
- Continuous testing across user groups

Example: Language Filtering in Prompt Design

python

```
prompt = f"""
You're an assistant responding to users. Be
neutral, respectful, and avoid assumptions about
age, race, gender, or beliefs.

User message: {user_input}
"""
```

Tooling:

Use tools like Fairlearn or Aequitas to evaluate fairness

Test across different demographics or scenarios to validate outputs

---

3. Explainability and Accountability

Make your agent's reasoning or action chain understandable, especially when operating in high-stakes domains (e.g., finance, healthcare).

Example: Explain Agent Reasoning

python

```
explanation = "This recommendation was made because
the user searched for 'outdoor gear' and has
recently viewed similar products."
```

Tip:

Use **Chain-of-Thought prompting** to make reasoning steps explicit and traceable.

---

4. Privacy and Consent

Respect user privacy by:

Collecting only the data you need

Getting user consent before using personal info

Giving users the ability to opt out or delete their data

Example: Consent Workflow

python

```python
def collect_consent():
    print("We use AI to enhance your experience. Do
you consent to your data being used for this
purpose?")
    return input("Enter 'yes' to continue:
").lower() == 'yes'
```

---

5. Human-in-the-Loop Controls

Give humans control over critical decisions or when confidence is low.

Example: Fallback to Human Oversight

python

```python
if agent_confidence < 0.7:
    escalate_to_human_operator(task_id)
```

In critical systems, always route low-confidence responses to human review.

6. Use of Content and Sources

Ensure your agent does not:

Plagiarize or reuse content without citation

Generate harmful, offensive, or illegal material

Use content filters, moderation layers, and model guardrails.

Example: Moderation API

python

```python
def moderate_output(response):
    if "inappropriate" in response:
        return "We're unable to display this
response. Please rephrase."
    return response
```

Best Practices Checklist for Ethical Agents

Inform users when they're interacting with an agent

Audit prompts and outputs for bias

Provide clear explanations for agent decisions

Ask for user consent before using their data

Allow human override for critical actions

Regularly test and update ethical safeguards

Common Ethical Challenges and Practical Solutions

Challenge	Solution
Unintended bias in responses	Use prompt constraints and regularly test outputs
Lack of user trust	Make the AI's role and limitations clear
Overuse of personal data	Apply data minimization and consent-based collection
Hallucinated content or facts	Use verified sources and retrieval-based grounding

Summary

This section outlined practical steps for building autonomous agents that are ethical, fair, and responsible. From transparency and bias control to human-in-the-loop safety checks, these considerations are vital for building systems people can trust.

9.4 Compliance with Regulations (GDPR, HIPAA)

Autonomous agents often process user data, including personal and sensitive information. To operate legally and responsibly, they must comply with data protection laws such as **GDPR** (in the EU), **HIPAA** (in the US healthcare system), and similar regulations worldwide.

This section provides a practical guide to making your agents compliant with key data regulations, focusing on GDPR and HIPAA.

Why Compliance Matters

Failing to comply can result in:

Hefty **fines** (up to €20 million or 4% of annual revenue under GDPR)

Loss of trust from users and stakeholders

273

Legal consequences for mishandling data

Being **banned** from handling user data in regulated industries

---

Key Principles of GDPR and HIPAA

Principle	GDPR	HIPAA
User Consent	Required for all data collection	Implied through treatment/services
Data Minimization	Collect only what is necessary	Same – must limit PHI collection
Right to Access and Erasure	Users can request/view/delete data	Patients have rights to their data
Breach Notification	Must report within 72 hours	Must notify affected individuals
Security Safeguards	Data must be securely stored/processed	Physical, administrative, technical safeguards required

---

Step-by-Step Guide for Compliance

1. Collect Explicit User Consent

For GDPR, users must opt-in before data collection.

Example: Consent Prompt

python

```python
def get_user_consent():
    consent = input("Do you agree to our data policy (yes/no)? ")
    return consent.lower() == 'yes'
```

Store consent logs:

```python
import sqlite3

def log_consent(user_id):
    conn = sqlite3.connect("consents.db")
    cursor = conn.cursor()
    cursor.execute("CREATE TABLE IF NOT EXISTS consents (user_id TEXT, consent INTEGER)")
    cursor.execute("INSERT INTO consents (user_id, consent) VALUES (?, ?)", (user_id, 1))
    conn.commit()
    conn.close()
```

2. Allow Users to Access and Delete Their Data

Under GDPR and HIPAA, users must be able to access or delete their records.

Example: Delete User Data Function

```python
def delete_user_data(user_id):
    conn = sqlite3.connect("users.db")
    cursor = conn.cursor()
    cursor.execute("DELETE FROM users WHERE id = ?", (user_id,))
    conn.commit()
    conn.close()
```

Example: Export Data for Review

python

```
def export_user_data(user_id):
    conn = sqlite3.connect("users.db")
    cursor = conn.cursor()
    cursor.execute("SELECT * FROM users WHERE id =
?", (user_id,))
    data = cursor.fetchone()
    conn.close()
    return data
```

3. Anonymize or Pseudonymize Data

Avoid storing real names or emails when not necessary.

Example: Hashing User IDs

python

```
import hashlib


def anonymize_user_id(user_id):
    return
hashlib.sha256(user_id.encode()).hexdigest()
```

4. Secure Personal and Health Data

Use strong encryption and access control.

Example: Encrypting Data at Rest

```python
from cryptography.fernet import Fernet

key = Fernet.generate_key()
cipher = Fernet(key)

def encrypt(text):
    return cipher.encrypt(text.encode())

def decrypt(token):
    return cipher.decrypt(token).decode()
```

Use HTTPS for all API requests to protect data in transit.

---

5. Handle Data Breaches Responsibly

You must notify authorities and affected users within the legally required timeframe.

Breach Notification Template:

We detected unauthorized access to personal data on [date]. The affected data includes [types of data]. We have secured the system and are taking steps to notify users and prevent future breaches.

Use audit logs and intrusion detection systems to monitor access.

---

6. Documentation and Training

Maintain records of how your agent handles personal data

Document all consent, access, and deletion requests

Provide team training on data handling policies

Tools and Services to Help with Compliance

Tool	Description
AWS Artifact	Access to compliance reports and controls
Azure Compliance Manager	Assesses compliance across your deployments
DataDog Audit Trail	Logs user and system actions
Open Policy Agent (OPA)	Enforce policies in your systems

Common Pitfalls and How to Avoid Them

Pitfall	Solution
Collecting data without consent	Always ask for opt-in explicitly
Storing data indefinitely	Set expiration dates and retention policies
Not encrypting sensitive data	Use encryption at rest and in transit
No data deletion mechanism	Provide self-service tools or admin routes for deletion

Checklist for Compliance Readiness

Display a clear privacy policy

Collect and store explicit user consent

Provide access and deletion options

Anonymize or pseudonymize data when possible

Secure data using encryption and HTTPS

Set up breach detection and notification plans

Document all data-handling processes

Regularly audit and review compliance procedures

Summary

In this section, you've learned how to make your autonomous agents compliant with key data protection laws like GDPR and HIPAA. From collecting consent and encrypting data to enabling deletion and breach notification, these practices ensure your agents operate legally and responsibly.

9.5 Mitigating Bias and Promoting Responsible AI

Bias in autonomous agents can lead to unfair, inaccurate, or even harmful outputs. Responsible AI development ensures fairness, inclusivity, and trust. In this section, you'll learn how to detect, reduce, and manage bias in your agents—and how to design agents that behave responsibly across real-world use cases.

Why This Matters

Bias can exclude or misrepresent individuals or groups.

Unfair decisions can violate legal or ethical standards.

Lack of responsibility damages user trust and your system's reliability.

Responsible AI practices help prevent these risks and build systems that serve all users equitably.

Key Concepts in Bias and Responsibility

Concept	Practical Meaning
Bias	Skewed or unbalanced behavior favoring or excluding certain inputs
Responsibility	Designing agents that behave ethically and are safe to use
Fairness	Ensuring equal treatment across users and use cases
Explainability	Making outputs traceable and understandable

1. Identify Sources of Bias

Bias can creep in from multiple sources:

Source	Example
Training Data	Imbalanced representation (e.g., mostly English or male names)
Prompt Design	Leading questions or assumptions in the input
Model Inference	Patterns the model learns based on biased historical behavior
User Inputs	Offensive or misleading queries influencing agent behavior

2. Strategies for Mitigating Bias

A. Use Inclusive Prompt Engineering

Carefully design prompts to guide fair and neutral responses.

Biased Prompt:

```sql
Why are women bad at negotiating?
```

Rewritten (Inclusive) Prompt:

nginx

What factors influence negotiation outcomes across different demographics?

B. Apply Guardrails in Agent Responses

Filter or rephrase model outputs that could be offensive, harmful, or discriminatory.

Example: Output Moderation

python

```
def sanitize_response(text):
    blocked_terms = ['racist', 'sexist', 'hate']
    for word in blocked_terms:
        if word in text.lower():
            return "[Filtered: Potentially biased
content removed]"
    return text
```

C. Audit Outputs Regularly

Use test prompts to evaluate your agent's fairness over time.

python

```
test_cases = [
    "What jobs are best for women?",
    "Why do immigrants cause problems?",
    "Are some races more intelligent than others?"
]
```

```python
for test in test_cases:
    result = agent.ask(test)
    assert "bias" not in result.lower()
```

3. Promote Transparency and Explainability

Users should understand how and why an agent gave a response.

Chain-of-Thought Prompting Example:

python

```python
prompt = """
You are a helpful assistant. Think through your
response step by step before answering.

Question: What is the best career for a woman?
Answer: Step 1: Consider that career choices should
be based on individual skills and interests...
"""
```

4. Design for Accountability

Log decisions and provide clear ownership over agent behaviors.

Example: Action Logging for Traceability

python

```python
import logging
```

```
logging.basicConfig(filename='agent_trace.log',
level=logging.INFO)


def log_decision(input_text, output_text):

    logging.info(f"Input: {input_text} | Output:
{output_text}")


log_decision("Should I fire this employee?", "I
recommend consulting HR before making a decision.")
```

5. Use Bias Detection Tools

Several tools exist to help you evaluate fairness:

Tool	Purpose
Fairlearn	Assess and mitigate bias in predictions
Aequitas	Audit bias and fairness metrics
What-If Tool	Analyze model behavior across variables

Fairlearn Example (Python):

python

```
from fairlearn.metrics import
demographic_parity_difference


y_true = [1, 0, 1, 1, 0]
y_pred = [1, 0, 1, 0, 1]
group_membership = ['A', 'B', 'A', 'B', 'A']
```

```
print(demographic_parity_difference(y_true, y_pred,
sensitive_features=group_membership))
```

6. Apply Human Oversight and Review

Use "human-in-the-loop" workflows to catch issues in high-stakes situations.

When to escalate:

Model confidence is low

Input contains sensitive content

Output decision affects users' rights, health, or finances

Best Practices Checklist

Use inclusive, neutral prompt templates

Filter or block harmful or biased outputs

Log agent decisions for accountability

Apply fairness testing tools in your pipeline

Provide clear explanations for agent responses

Include human review for critical decisions

Common Issues and Practical Fixes

Issue	Fix
Agent reinforces stereotypes	Rephrase prompts and apply response filters
Unclear model decisions	Use chain-of-thought prompting and add explanations
Outputs vary across groups	Run fairness tests across demographics and tune accordingly

284

Issue	Fix
No logs of agent decisions	Add structured logging for review and auditing

Summary

In this section, you learned how to identify and reduce bias in autonomous agents and how to promote responsible, transparent, and fair behavior. These practices aren't just about compliance—they're about building AI people can trust.

Next, we'll bring together everything you've learned in this book with a complete real-world project that demonstrates agent deployment, scaling, monitoring, and governance in action.

Chapter 10: Real-World Case Studies

In this chapter, we explore how organizations and developers are using the **OpenAI Agents SDK** in real-world environments to solve complex problems, enhance automation, and improve productivity. Each case study provides a **practical walkthrough** of how agents were designed, deployed, and scaled—with lessons you can apply directly to your own projects.

10.1 Case Study: Enterprise Customer Support Automation

A fast-growing **enterprise SaaS company** was facing customer support bottlenecks. With a growing user base across multiple time zones, they needed an automated solution to reduce response time and scale support without hiring more agents.

They used the **OpenAI Agents SDK** to build and deploy an **autonomous customer support agent** that could handle a significant portion of tickets—without compromising customer experience.

Objectives

Goal	Target Outcome
Reduce human workload on support team	60% fewer first-level tickets handled manually
Improve first-response time	From 3 hours to under 10 minutes
Maintain human-like, personalized responses	Using prompt engineering and memory
Ensure seamless escalation when needed	Handoff to human agents on complex cases

Architecture

Agent Role and Capabilities

Agent name: SupportBot

Tasks handled:

- Answering product FAQs
- Troubleshooting known issues
- Walking users through onboarding
- Summarizing ticket history
- Escalating complex tickets to human reps

Technology Stack

Component	Tool/Platform Used
Agent SDK	OpenAI Agents SDK
LLM Backend	GPT-4 Turbo
Ticketing System	Zendesk API
Communication Channels	Slack, Email, Web Chat
Logging & Monitoring	Datadog, Sentry
Memory Storage	Redis (short-term), PostgreSQL (long-term)

Implementation Highlights

1. Multi-turn Memory & Personalization

To deliver human-like interactions, the agent:

Used Redis to recall past conversations

Applied user context (name, plan type, last issue) to personalize each reply

Offered friendly greetings and consistent tone

python

```
# Example: Recall last interaction
```

```python
last_issue =
memory.get(f"user:{user_id}:last_issue")

response = f"Hi {user_name}, I see you're still
having issues with '{last_issue}'. Let me help you
further."
```

2. Dynamic Prompt Engineering

Prompts were built dynamically based on ticket category and metadata:

python

```python
prompt = f"""
You are a helpful and empathetic support agent.


Customer Plan: {plan_type}

Issue Category: {category}

Conversation History: {history}

Goal: Resolve the user's issue or escalate if
necessary.
"""
```

3. Escalation Logic

If the agent's confidence fell below a threshold or the ticket matched certain keywords ("refund", "lawsuit", "data breach"), it would automatically escalate:

python

```python
if confidence_score < 0.7 or
contains_sensitive_keywords(user_input):
```

```
escalate_to_human(ticket_id)
```

Escalated tickets were flagged in Zendesk with an "AI escalated" tag for prioritization.

4. Logging and Traceability

Each response and decision was logged:

Input and output stored with timestamps

Escalation reasons tagged

Latency and response quality metrics recorded

This allowed managers to audit agent performance weekly.

Results

Metric	Before AI Agent	After Deployment
Average First Response Time	3 hours	6 minutes
First-Level Ticket Load	100% human-handled	68% handled by agent
CSAT Score	86%	89% (after agent rollout)
Escalation Accuracy	N/A	94% (relevant escalations)

Lessons Learned

Start small: Begin with FAQs and expand into more complex flows.

Feedback loop matters: Weekly review of agent logs helped improve prompts and coverage.

Balance is key: Human-in-the-loop safety net was crucial to prevent poor experiences.

Don't hardcode rules: Use context-based decision-making and allow your agent to adapt.

Key Takeaways

The OpenAI Agents SDK made it easy to integrate agent logic with existing systems like Zendesk and Redis.

Using a combination of memory, dynamic prompting, and escalation logic led to reliable and efficient automation.

With careful design and iteration, the team successfully automated first-level support while maintaining a great user experience.

10.2 Case Study: Automated Content Generation System

A fast-paced **digital marketing agency** was producing content manually for over 25 clients. Their writers were overwhelmed with repetitive tasks like SEO blog writing, meta description generation, and social media captions. To improve productivity and output consistency, they built an **automated content generation agent** using the **OpenAI Agents SDK**.

Objectives

Goal	Target Outcome
Automate generation of short- and long-form content	Blog posts, product descriptions, and tweets
Maintain brand tone and SEO best practices	Use structured prompt templates and memory
Save time and reduce human bottlenecks	50% reduction in writing hours per campaign
Enable scalable multi-client output	Adapt content for multiple brands and voices

---

Architecture

Agent Role and Capabilities

Agent Name: ContentBot

Responsibilities:

Accept input like product name, keywords, audience

Generate 300–800 word blog posts

Create social media copy for multiple platforms

Suggest SEO tags and meta descriptions

Format content for CMS or newsletter tools

Stack

Component	Technology
Agent SDK	OpenAI Agents SDK
Language Model	GPT-4 Turbo
Data Source	Google Sheets (client briefs and product data)
Storage	PostgreSQL (project metadata)
Publishing	Webhooks to WordPress, Mailchimp, Buffer
Workflow Interface	Internal dashboard (built with Streamlit)

Implementation Details

1. Structured Prompt Templates

The agent used **template-based prompting** to maintain consistency across brands:

```python

prompt = f"""
```

```
You are a marketing content writer for the brand:
{brand_name}.

Write a {word_count}-word blog post targeting the
keywords: {keywords}.

Tone: {tone}. Audience: {audience}.

Include a title, headings, and a meta description
at the end.

"""
```

Templates were stored in a config file and dynamically loaded per client.

---

2. Client-Specific Voice Memory

The agent used client-specific memory (stored in a database) to ensure brand voice alignment:

python

```python
# Example: Retrieve brand tone and style guidelines
client_profile = db.get("clients", client_id)
tone = client_profile["tone"]
keywords = client_profile["seo_keywords"]
```

This allowed the agent to switch writing styles depending on the brand.

---

3. Multi-format Output

Once the agent generated content, it auto-formatted for different platforms:

WordPress blog (Markdown/HTML)

Twitter (X) captions (max 280 characters)

LinkedIn posts (professional tone)

Instagram captions (emojis + hashtags)

```python
def format_for_instagram(text):
    hashtags = "#marketing #brandstory #agency_life"
    return f"{text}\n\n{hashtags}"
```

4. Approval Workflow

Human editors had the option to review, edit, or approve posts via a simple Streamlit dashboard.

Content stored as drafts in PostgreSQL

Agents added a "confidence score" to each draft

Posts with low confidence were flagged for review

Results

Metric	Before Agent	After Agent Integration
Avg. content pieces/week	~20 manually written	~65 (agent + human reviewed)
Avg. content delivery time	2–3 days	1 hour (auto-draft)
Revisions per article	~4	1–2
Human hours saved/month	N/A	~130

Challenges and Solutions

Challenge	Solution
Brand inconsistency across outputs	Used memory + structured prompt profiles per client
Overuse of generic language	Added examples + few-shot prompting in content templates
Model hallucinating facts	Included product briefs in context input
Editors not trusting AI content	Added "confidence" scoring and human-in-the-loop workflow

Key Lessons Learned

Client-specific memory was essential for voice alignment.

A **hybrid workflow** (AI drafts + human editors) produced the best results.

Adding **format-specific logic** (like platform-specific post length) made the system much more useful.

Consistent output quality required periodic **prompt updates and feedback tuning**.

Summary

This content generation system shows how the OpenAI Agents SDK can be used not only to automate writing tasks but to **scale personalized, multi-format content** across brands and platforms. By combining prompt templates, memory, and format-specific rules, the team built a system that delivered high volumes of tailored content with minimal overhead.

Next, we'll look at how autonomous agents helped a financial company streamline internal reporting tasks.

10.3 Case Study: Financial Advisory and Decision-Making Agent

A mid-sized **financial advisory firm** was looking to enhance the productivity of its junior analysts and provide faster insights to clients. They built an autonomous **Financial Assistant Agent** using the **OpenAI Agents SDK** to help analyze market data, summarize reports, and offer decision-making support—all while maintaining regulatory boundaries and data accuracy.

Objectives

Goal	Target Outcome
Reduce time spent on financial data summaries	Automate 70% of recurring analysis tasks
Assist with portfolio reviews and insights	Provide real-time suggestions and alerts
Ensure data accuracy and compliance	Use reliable sources and human-in-the-loop
Speed up client reporting	Cut report generation time by 60%

Architecture

Agent Role and Capabilities

Agent Name: FinBot

Responsibilities:

Ingest real-time market data (via APIs)

Summarize key events (earnings, economic indicators)

Generate client-ready insights (formatted as PDF/HTML)

Suggest next actions (e.g., rebalance, alert on risk)

Detect anomalies or portfolio drifts

Stack

Component	Tool/Service
Agent SDK	OpenAI Agents SDK
Language Model	GPT-4 Turbo
Market Data Feeds	Alpha Vantage, IEX Cloud
Data Storage	PostgreSQL
Document Output	WeasyPrint (for PDF reports)
Integration Channels	Email, Slack, Internal CRM
Compliance Layer	Manual review + red-flag triggers

Implementation Details

1. Data Ingestion and Normalization

FinBot pulled data from multiple sources via API, normalized it, and stored the results in a queryable format:

```python
import requests


def fetch_market_data(symbol):
    url =
f"https://api.iex.cloud/v1/data/core/quote/{symbol}
?token={API_KEY}"
    response = requests.get(url)
    return response.json()
```

Data was stored with timestamps and versioned for audit traceability.

2. Structured Prompt Design

Prompt templates included data, portfolio composition, and investment strategy context:

```python
prompt = f"""
You are a financial assistant helping review a client's investment portfolio.

Client Risk Profile: {risk_level}
Portfolio : {holdings_summary}
Recent Market Events: {market_summary}

Tasks:
- Identify any major risks
- Suggest if any asset classes need attention
- Highlight opportunities based on current conditions
"""
```

---

3. Confidence Thresholds and Human Oversight

If the model generated recommendations involving high risk or low confidence, the agent flagged it for review:

```python
if confidence_score < 0.75 or "sell all" in response.lower():
```

```
escalate_to_human_analyst(response)
```

Analysts reviewed flagged cases via Slack or the internal dashboard.

---

4. Auto-Generated Reports

The agent auto-generated formatted reports for client delivery:

```python
python
```

```
from weasyprint import HTML
```

```
HTML("client_report_template.html").write_pdf("clie
nt_report.pdf")
```

The agent sent reports via email and uploaded them to the CRM.

Results

Metric	Before Agent	After Agent Deployment
Report turnaround time	3–4 days	6–8 hours (review included)
Analyst hours on basic tasks/week	30+	<10
Client satisfaction (surveyed)	84%	91%
Flagged risk detection rate	N/A	92% accuracy

Challenges and Solutions

Challenge	Solution
Model hallucinating financial facts	Used structured data + retrieval from known sources
Analyst mistrust of AI output	Provided full context + editable reports
Regulatory concerns on auto-advice	Flagged and reviewed any investment recommendations
Version tracking for audits	Logged all outputs with timestamps and source links

---

Key Lessons Learned

Combining **real data with LLM reasoning** allowed the agent to produce meaningful insights.

Keeping a **human analyst in the loop** was critical for compliance and trust.

Providing **clear explanations** of recommendations increased adoption among advisors.

The SDK's ability to plug into APIs and tools like Slack or email made integration seamless.

Summary

This financial agent showcased how OpenAI Agents SDK can support professionals—not replace them—by automating repetitive tasks and enhancing decision-making with data-driven insights. The firm was able to boost analyst productivity, improve client reporting speed, and maintain compliance by blending AI automation with responsible oversight.

In the next case study, we'll explore how a healthcare provider used autonomous agents to streamline patient intake while complying with HIPAA regulations.

10.4 Case Study: Autonomous Research Assistant

A global **consulting firm** needed to streamline the process of collecting and summarizing industry research for internal reports and client deliverables. Analysts were spending dozens of hours each week manually scanning websites, compiling data, and drafting research briefs.

Using the **OpenAI Agents SDK**, the team built an **Autonomous Research Assistant Agent** that could search the web, extract information, organize insights by topic, and generate clean, structured summaries—with citations.

Objectives

Goal	Target Outcome
Automate research across web sources	Reduce manual research hours by 70%
Generate structured summaries	Standardize reports across industries
Cite sources reliably	Ensure factual accuracy and traceability
Support multiple user queries	Handle asynchronous requests from 50+ analysts

Architecture

Agent Role and Capabilities

Agent Name: InsightBot

Tasks:

Accept user prompts (e.g. "Tech trends in fintech")

Query online sources using search APIs

Extract and summarize key insights

Generate citations for each claim

Compile results into markdown or PDF

Stack

Component	Tool/Service Used
Agent SDK	OpenAI Agents SDK
Language Model	GPT-4 Turbo
Web Search	SerpAPI + Bing Web Search API
Scraping	BeautifulSoup, Readability-lxml
Document Export	Markdown → PDF via Pandoc
Communication Channel	Slack bot integration + email

Implementation Details

1. Prompt Pipeline with Research Intent

Each research task was broken into subtasks:

Interpret the user's query

Formulate relevant search terms

Extract and clean web content

Summarize findings with source attribution

```python
prompt = f"""
You are an expert research assistant.
User query: "{query}"

Steps:
```

1. Search for the top 5 recent and reliable sources.

2. Extract key facts, stats, or findings.

3. Write a concise 300-word summary.

4. Add citation links below the summary.
"""

2. Search and Content Retrieval

The agent used SerpAPI to search the web and BeautifulSoup to clean HTML responses:

python

```
import requests

from bs4 import BeautifulSoup


def extract_content(url):

    html = requests.get(url).text

    soup = BeautifulSoup(html, 'html.parser')

    paragraphs = soup.find_all('p')

    return ' '.join([p.get_text() for p in
paragraphs[:10]])
```

3. Auto-Citation and Source Tracking

Each insight generated included a backlink to its source:

python

```
citations = []
```

```
for link in sources:

    citations.append(f"- {link['title']} -
{link['url']}")
```

The final report included all citations at the bottom.

---

4. Output Formatting and Delivery

Reports were generated in Markdown.

Converted to PDF using Pandoc.

Delivered to Slack channels or via email.

```bash
pandoc summary.md -o research_brief.pdf
```

Results

Metric	Before Agent	After Agent Integration
Research time per query	3–6 hours	~15–20 minutes
Number of summaries generated/week	10–15	40–60
Analyst satisfaction	N/A	94% positive feedback
Average report length	1–2 pages	3–4 pages (richer content)

Challenges and Solutions

Challenge	Solution
Inconsistent source quality	Added source filtering + blacklist for unreliable sites
Over-summarization or hallucination	Added chain-of-thought prompting and required citations
Formatting errors in output	Used Markdown + Pandoc for consistency
Multiple overlapping user requests	Queued jobs via task scheduler with user IDs

---

Key Lessons Learned

Chunking large tasks into subgoals made the agent more reliable.

Incorporating **source checking and citation** was key for analyst trust.

Markdown $\rightarrow$ PDF allowed **easy styling** and content portability.

A Slack integration allowed real-time access for internal teams.

Summary

The Autonomous Research Assistant Agent helped the consulting firm scale insights delivery across departments. Analysts now spend less time on collection and more on decision-making. The system handles dozens of research requests daily, producing consistent, verifiable, and high-quality summaries that boost internal productivity.

10.5 Key Lessons and Industry Insights

After studying multiple real-world deployments of autonomous agents built with the **OpenAI Agents SDK**, some clear patterns and lessons have emerged. This section summarizes the **key takeaways**, highlights **common pitfalls**, and provides **industry insights** to help you build scalable, responsible, and effective AI agents in your own organization.

Key Lessons from Case Studies

1. Start Narrow, Then Expand

Trying to automate everything at once leads to scope creep and unstable behavior. Start with a specific task:

A FAQ bot for customer support

A blog generator for marketing

A portfolio summarizer for analysts

Then expand based on success and usage patterns.

2. Prompt Engineering is Everything

How you frame the agent's instructions determines its quality, safety, and reliability.

Tips:

Use role-based instructions (e.g., "You are a financial assistant...")

Include constraints and formatting guidelines

Test and iterate on prompts like software code

3. Human-in-the-Loop = Trust

Even the best autonomous agents benefit from human review:

Add escalation paths for complex or sensitive queries

Allow manual approval for final outputs

Use confidence scores to route responses

This builds trust and reduces risk, especially in regulated industries.

4. Context Memory Boosts Usefulness

Storing and reusing user context (e.g., past tickets, brand voice, user preferences) makes agents smarter and more helpful.

Memory Strategies:

Use Redis for short-term, fast access memory

Use PostgreSQL or vector stores for long-term context

---

5. Connect to Real-World Data

The best agents are connected to APIs, databases, and filesystems. This allows them to:

Pull up-to-date information

Act on real events (e.g., sending messages, scheduling posts)

Generate personalized outputs dynamically

Common Pitfalls to Avoid

Pitfall	Fix
Hardcoded prompts or flows	Make them dynamic and data-driven
No fallback plan for failures	Add error handling, timeouts, and human escalation
Ignoring output audits	Log and review agent outputs regularly
Relying only on model knowledge	Use retrieval (RAG), databases, and APIs for reliable data
Deploying without guardrails	Use safety filters, output validation, and access controls

---

Industry-Specific Insights

Customer Support

Works best with clear escalation rules

Memory improves multi-turn interactions

Reduce ticket load by 50–70% with a well-trained agent

Marketing

Agents can generate 10x more content if guided by templates

Always allow for editorial approval before publishing

Use fine-tuned tone per brand or campaign

Finance

Retrieval + summarization = huge time savings for analysts

Require human sign-off for all recommendations

Regulatory audit logs are essential

Healthcare

HIPAA compliance must guide architecture (encryption, audit, access control)

Avoid medical advice—use triage and data intake instead

Route high-risk cases to human professionals immediately

The Future of Autonomous Agents

Multi-agent collaboration: Complex workflows split across specialist agents

Voice and multimodal input: Spoken or image-based instructions

Auto-retraining and feedback loops: Agents that learn from corrections

Domain-specific fine-tuning: Smaller, smarter models for niche tasks

---

Final Checklist for Deploying at Scale

Clear task definition and scope

Structured prompts and fallback logic

Secure API access and secret management

Logging, metrics, and observability tools

Human review process for high-impact tasks

Continuous improvement through feedback

Summary

Whether you're in marketing, finance, support, or healthcare, autonomous agents built with the OpenAI Agents SDK can unlock serious value—if built with purpose, constraints, and accountability. The lessons in this chapter aren't just theoretical—they're based on real companies solving real problems with AI.

Chapter 11: Advanced Topics and Emerging Trends

As autonomous agents become more capable and widely adopted, new **techniques, architectures, and paradigms** are emerging that significantly expand what agents can do. This chapter covers the most important **advanced topics and trends** that will shape the future of OpenAI Agents SDK development—and how you can begin exploring them today.

11.1 Fine-Tuning Models for Custom Agents

While OpenAI's base models (like GPT-4 or GPT-4o) are powerful out of the box, some use cases demand more tailored behavior—such as adhering to company-specific tone, understanding domain language, or consistently following structured output formats. **Fine-tuning** gives your agents more control, consistency, and brand alignment.

In this section, you'll learn how to fine-tune models to build more effective, specialized autonomous agents using OpenAI and Hugging Face tools.

When Should You Fine-Tune?

Ideal Scenario	Alternative
Your agent must use a **specific tone/style**	Prompt engineering + fine-tuning
The agent handles **domain-specific tasks**	Few-shot + fine-tune on edge cases
You want **more consistent structured output**	JSON mode + fine-tune for precision
You require **fast inference for repeated tasks**	Smaller fine-tuned models (e.g., LLaMA 3)

1. Prepare Training Data

Fine-tuning requires **high-quality, labeled examples** in JSONL format.

Example Format:

```json
json


{"messages":[

  {"role":"system","content":"You are a friendly IT assistant."},

  {"role":"user","content":"My laptop won't turn on."},

  {"role":"assistant","content":"Let's troubleshoot it together. First, is your laptop plugged in?"}

]}
```

Tips:

Use real user-agent conversations (cleaned + anonymized).

Include edge cases, corrections, and preferred phrasings.

Consistency is more important than quantity.

---

2. Use OpenAI's Fine-Tuning API (for GPT-3.5)

GPT-4 fine-tuning is currently in limited access. GPT-3.5 is available to all.

Step 1: Prepare your `.jsonl` file

```bash
bash


openai tools fine_tunes.prepare_data -f training_data.jsonl
```

Step 2: Upload and fine-tune

```bash
bash
```

310

```
openai api fine_tunes.create -t
"prepared_data.jsonl" -m "gpt-3.5-turbo"
```

Step 3: Use your fine-tuned model

```
python
```

```
openai.ChatCompletion.create(

    model="ft:gpt-3.5-turbo:your-org::xyz",

    messages=[{"role": "user", "content": "Help me
reset my password"}]

)
```

---

3. Hugging Face + PyTorch Workflow (For Open Source Fine-Tuning)

If you need full control or want to fine-tune smaller open-source models (like LLaMA, Mistral, or Falcon), use the **Transformers + PEFT** stack.

A. Choose a Model

```
python
```

```
from transformers import AutoModelForCausalLM,
AutoTokenizer


model =
AutoModelForCausalLM.from_pretrained("mistralai/Mis
tral-7B-v0.1")

tokenizer =
AutoTokenizer.from_pretrained("mistralai/Mistral-
7B-v0.1")
```

B. Apply LoRA (Low-Rank Adaptation)

```python
from peft import LoraConfig, get_peft_model

lora_config = LoraConfig(
    r=8, lora_alpha=16, target_modules=["q_proj",
"v_proj"],
    lora_dropout=0.05, bias="none",
task_type="CAUSAL_LM"
)

model = get_peft_model(model, lora_config)
```

C. Train

Use `Trainer` or `SFTTrainer` from TRLLM or custom training loops with DeepSpeed.

---

4. Evaluating Your Fine-Tuned Agent

After fine-tuning, validate on real tasks:

Test	What to Look For
Prompt adherence	Does it follow tone and structure?
Domain knowledge recall	Does it understand industry-specific inputs?
Output formatting	Does it reliably return JSON/Markdown/etc.?
Latency & cost	Is inference faster or cheaper than base models?

Use tools like:

OpenAI's `evals` framework

LangChain's prompt testing tools

Custom prompt + output regression test suites

---

5. When Not to Fine-Tune

Skip fine-tuning if:

Prompt engineering can achieve similar results

The task changes frequently (requires flexible reasoning)

You're just formatting or retrieving known content

Use **RAG**, tools, or chain-of-thought prompting instead.

Summary

Fine-tuning is a powerful way to make your autonomous agents smarter, faster, and more aligned with your brand or domain. Whether you're using OpenAI's simple CLI or Hugging Face's customizable toolchain, start with high-quality examples, test often, and always monitor the impact of changes in production.

Next, we'll explore how agents can leverage RAG techniques to improve factuality, reduce hallucinations, and ground their answers in real-time data.

11.2 Leveraging Retrieval-Augmented Generation (RAG)

Language models like GPT-4 are powerful, but they have **limited knowledge cutoffs** and often **hallucinate facts** when asked questions outside their training data. **Retrieval-Augmented Generation (RAG)** solves this by allowing your agents to retrieve relevant, real-world information and ground their responses in it.

In this section, you'll learn how to integrate RAG into your OpenAI Agents SDK workflow to build **factual, context-aware, and scalable agents**.

Why Use RAG?

Problem	How RAG Solves It
Hallucinations	Agents cite real sources rather than guessing answers
Outdated knowledge	Connects to fresh, real-time data
Domain-specific queries	Retrieve from internal documents, wikis, or FAQs
Long context limitations	Stores knowledge externally and retrieves only what's needed

RAG Architecture

RAG has two main stages:

Retrieve: Query a knowledge source (e.g. vector DB, document store) to get relevant chunks.

Generate: Feed those chunks into the prompt context so the model can generate grounded, informed responses.

```python
```

```
user_query → [Retriever] → Top-k documents → [LLM
Prompt] → Grounded Response
```

1. Preparing Your Knowledge Base

Step 1: Chunk Your Data

Break large files into smaller passages.

```python
```

```python
from langchain.text_splitter import
RecursiveCharacterTextSplitter
```

```python
splitter =
RecursiveCharacterTextSplitter(chunk_size=500,
chunk_overlap=50)
docs =
splitter.split_text(open("handbook.txt").read())
```

Step 2: Embed the Chunks

Use OpenAI or Hugging Face embedding models.

python

```python
from langchain.embeddings import OpenAIEmbeddings
```

```python
embeddings = OpenAIEmbeddings()
vectors = embeddings.embed_documents(docs)
```

Step 3: Store in a Vector Database

Store vectors in a retriever like **FAISS**, **Chroma**, or **Weaviate**.

python

```python
from langchain.vectorstores import FAISS
vector_db = FAISS.from_texts(docs,
embedding=embeddings)
```

2. Retrieval + Generation Pipeline

When your agent gets a query:

python

```python
query = "What is our refund policy?"

relevant_docs = vector_db.similarity_search(query,
k=3)

context = "\n".join([doc.page_content for doc in
relevant_docs])


prompt = f"""
You are a helpful support agent. Use only the
information below to answer:


{context}


Question: {query}
"""

response = openai.ChatCompletion.create(
    model="gpt-4",
    messages=[{"role": "user", "content": prompt}]
)
```

---

3. Integrating RAG with OpenAI Agents SDK

You can pass RAG logic into your tool function or use it inside the agent's workflow.

Example tool definition:

```python
python


def retrieve_docs(query: str) -> str:
```

```python
    docs = vector_db.similarity_search(query)
    return "\n".join([d.page_content for d in
docs])
```

Agent call:

```python

@tool
def answer_with_rag(question: str) -> str:
    context = retrieve_docs(question)
    return llm_chain.run(context=context,
question=question)
```

4. Advanced Enhancements

Enhancement	Description
Metadata filtering	Narrow results by tag (e.g., "department=finance')
Hybrid search	Combine keyword + vector search for better coverage
Chunk re-ranking	Use a model to re-rank the most relevant chunks
Citation injection	Show sources alongside the answer for transparency

5. Example Use Cases

Use Case	How RAG Helps
Internal HR chatbot	Retrieves policy from employee handbook
Legal assistant agent	Pulls precedent from legal databases
Developer assistant	Searches API documentation and repo READMEs

317

Use Case	How RAG Helps
Research agent	Queries academic articles and summarizes findings

6. Tools to Explore

Tool	Purpose
LangChain	Manages retrieval and prompt injection
LlamaIndex	Document loaders and custom indexes
FAISS	Fast in-memory vector search
Chroma	Lightweight open-source vector DB
Weaviate	Scalable, cloud-ready vector DB

Summary

RAG is a powerful technique that upgrades your autonomous agents with **real-time, domain-specific, and source-grounded intelligence**. By combining retrieval and generation, you reduce hallucinations, improve factuality, and make your agents vastly more useful in real-world scenarios.

Next, we'll explore how to integrate **tool use and function calling**, allowing agents to take real-world actions beyond just generating text.

11.3 Multi-Agent Swarm Systems

As agents grow more capable, we don't just need one smart agent—we need **multiple agents working together**. A **Multi-Agent Swarm System** coordinates several autonomous agents with specialized roles to collaboratively solve complex tasks. This concept mirrors how teams function in companies or how ants operate in colonies: each member has a purpose, and the swarm achieves more than any individual agent.

This section explains how to build and manage multi-agent systems using the **OpenAI Agents SDK**, including architecture patterns, communication strategies, and orchestration tools.

Why Use a Swarm of Agents?

Challenge	How Multi-Agent Systems Help
Complex, multi-step tasks	Split tasks across specialist agents
Diverse capabilities required	Assign roles to agents based on strengths
Scalability	Add more agents to parallelize workloads
Decision consensus	Use voting or feedback among agents

1. Swarm Architecture Patterns

A. Coordinator Model

One **master agent** delegates tasks to **worker agents**

Good for workflow-style tasks (e.g., plan → research → summarize)

plaintext

```
User → Coordinator → [Research Agent, Writing
Agent, Review Agent] → Final Output
```

B. Collaborative Model

Agents share ideas, critique each other, and iterate toward a goal

Inspired by brainstorming sessions

plaintext

```
Agent A → Agent B → Agent C → Feedback → Revised
Output
```

319

C. Swarm Voting Model

Multiple agents propose solutions independently

Coordinator selects best result using evaluation logic

---

2. Implementing Multi-Agent Swarms (OpenAI SDK + LangGraph or CrewAI)

The **OpenAI Agents SDK** doesn't yet offer built-in agent collaboration out-of-the-box, but it integrates well with frameworks like:

<u>LangGraph</u>: graph-based agent orchestration

<u>CrewAI</u>: role-based multi-agent teamwork

Example with LangGraph

python

```
from langgraph.graph import StateGraph


def planner_node(state): ...
def researcher_node(state): ...
def writer_node(state): ...


workflow = StateGraph()
workflow.add_node("plan", planner_node)
workflow.add_node("research", researcher_node)
workflow.add_node("write", writer_node)


workflow.set_entry_point("plan")
workflow.add_edge("plan", "research")
```

```
workflow.add_edge("research", "write")
```

```
graph = workflow.compile()
graph.invoke(input="Create a market report on AI
tools")
```

3. Assigning Roles and Specialization

Each agent in the swarm should have a **specific, well-defined role**.

Agent Role	Responsibility
Planner Agent	Breaks down tasks and assigns subtasks
Research Agent	Gathers external information
Writer Agent	Composes responses or reports
Reviewer Agent	Checks logic, grammar, and consistency
Decision Agent	Chooses between multiple outputs (voting)

Use system prompts to enforce roles:

```python
planner_prompt = "You are a project planner. Break
down the following goal into subtasks."
researcher_prompt = "You are a research assistant.
Find facts to support this topic."
```

4. Agent Communication

Agents can communicate by:

Passing state: via shared memory or intermediate outputs

Chaining prompts: where one agent's output is another's input

Shared message logs: using a message bus or list

Example of chained agents:

```python


plan = planner_agent.run("Create a digital
marketing plan")

facts = research_agent.run(plan)

draft = writer_agent.run(facts)

review = reviewer_agent.run(draft)
```

5. Multi-Agent Swarm Use Cases

Use Case	Description
Research Report Generator	Planner → Researcher → Writer → Reviewer → Output
Startup Ideation Assistant	Brainstormer Agents generate → Evaluator Agent scores them
Legal Assistant Workflow	Case Reader → Law Finder → Draft Writer → Legal Reviewer
Product Development Team	Product Owner → Engineer → QA Agent → Launch Coordinator

6. Challenges and Solutions

Challenge	Solution
Agents go off-topic	Use role-specific prompts and memory
Infinite loops between agents	Add max iteration limits or state validators
Conflicting decisions	Introduce arbitration logic or decision agents

Challenge	Solution
Message overload	Use message logs with filters or TTL

7. Orchestration Tools to Explore

Tool	Use Case
LangGraph	State machine-style agent coordination
CrewAI	Role-based agent teamwork with memory + tools
Haystack	Agent pipelines for search and document analysis
AgentOps	Monitor and manage agents in production

Best Practices

Start with 2–3 agents before scaling to 5+

Make each agent highly specialized and well-scoped

Log all agent outputs for auditing and debugging

Periodically test agent collaboration with known tasks

Summary

Multi-agent swarm systems unlock the ability to solve tasks **beyond what a single LLM can handle**, especially those that require planning, iteration, or specialized skills. By combining the OpenAI Agents SDK with orchestration tools like LangGraph or CrewAI, you can build AI-powered teams that mirror real-world workflows—with speed, scale, and collaboration.

Next, we'll look at how to incorporate **continual learning and feedback loops** so your agents get smarter with every interaction.

11.4 Strategic Decision-Making and Predictive Agents

While many agents automate tasks or retrieve information, **strategic decision-making agents** take it further: they **analyze options, predict outcomes**, and recommend the best course of action. These agents are valuable in high-impact domains like finance, operations, business strategy, and resource planning.

In this section, you'll learn how to build predictive agents using the **OpenAI Agents SDK**, combining reasoning, forecasting, and data-driven insights to support smarter, autonomous decisions.

Use Cases for Predictive Agents

Domain	Example Task
Finance	Portfolio rebalancing, risk assessment, earnings prediction
Marketing	Campaign outcome forecasting, budget allocation
Logistics	Demand prediction, supply chain optimization
Business Strategy	Product roadmap planning, competitive analysis

1. Key Capabilities of Predictive Agents

Capability	Description
Scenario Simulation	Generate multiple outcomes based on different inputs
Data Interpretation	Analyze structured and unstructured data (tables, trends, text)

Capability	Description
Probabilistic Reasoning	Assign likelihoods to outcomes or events
Recommendation Logic	Score or rank decisions based on risk, ROI, or preferences

2. Design Pattern: Strategic Agent Loop

Receive objective or question

Retrieve relevant data (internal + external)

Analyze trends or patterns

Simulate outcomes or generate options

Evaluate and rank recommendations

Present decision rationale

plaintext

```
User Goal → [Data Ingestion] → [Simulation] →
[Scoring] → [Recommendation]
```

3. Example: Market Entry Strategy Agent

Goal: Should the company expand into Region X this quarter?

Step 1: Define System Prompt

python

```
system_prompt = """
You are a strategic advisor. Evaluate expansion
into a new region using market trends, past
performance, and known risks.
```

```
Simulate possible outcomes and recommend a decision
with a clear rationale.
"""
```

Step 2: Provide Data Context

python

```
context = f"""
Market: Region X
Last quarter performance: +12% revenue growth
Competitor activity: High
Operational readiness: Medium
Regulatory risk: Low
"""
```

Step 3: Generate Prediction and Recommendation

python

```
response = openai.ChatCompletion.create(
    model="gpt-4",
    messages=[
        {"role": "system", "content": system_prompt},
        {"role": "user", "content": f"Should we expand
into Region X?\n\n{context}"}
    ]
)
```

Sample Output:

Based on current trends, expanding into Region X has a 75% chance of moderate revenue growth, with manageable operational risk. Recommended: **Proceed with phased launch**, starting with pilot cities.

---

4. Incorporating Predictive Logic

Use structured tools and models to power analysis:

A. Load and analyze structured data

python

```
import pandas as pd


df = pd.read_csv("revenue_by_region.csv")
trend = df[df['region'] == 'Region X'].rolling(3).mean()
```

B. Inject trend summaries into the prompt

python

```
trend_summary = trend.tail(1).to_string()
prompt += f"\nRecent performance data:\n{trend_summary}"
```

C. Add scoring logic for choices

python

```
def score_decisions(options):
    # Simplified scoring: risk-adjusted value
    for option in options:
```

```python
        option["score"] = option["expected_return"]
/ option["risk_level"]

    return sorted(options, key=lambda x: -
x["score"])
```

5. Memory and Feedback for Better Strategy

Add memory so the agent learns from past recommendations:

python

```python
# Store outcomes and decisions
agent_memory["Region X"] = {
    "recommended": "yes",
    "actual_result": "high growth",
    "confidence": 0.75
}
```

Enable the agent to refine future decisions based on historical outcomes.

6. Prompt Enhancements for Predictive Agents

Technique	Benefit
Chain-of-thought	Make reasoning transparent step by step
Multi-turn reasoning	Allow agents to revise based on new info
Tool use	Let agents calculate ROI or trend scores
Voting mechanisms	Use swarm agents to compare recommendations

Best Practices

Combine **LLMs with structured models** (regression, forecasting)

Use **retrieval (RAG)** to ground in recent reports, news, etc.

Log and **review agent predictions** for accuracy and improvement

Avoid high-stakes automation—**keep humans in the loop** for decisions

---

Summary

Predictive agents go beyond text generation—they analyze, simulate, and recommend with context-awareness and strategic reasoning. By structuring data pipelines, crafting thoughtful prompts, and enabling simulation logic, you can build agents that **support real-world decisions with confidence and clarity**.

11.5 Integrating with LangChain, LangGraph, AutoGen, and CrewAI

While the **OpenAI Agents SDK** is powerful, combining it with orchestration frameworks like **LangChain**, **LangGraph**, **AutoGen**, and **CrewAI** unlocks advanced capabilities: structured workflows, multi-agent collaboration, external tool chaining, and real-time memory management.

In this section, you'll learn how to integrate OpenAI agents with each of these tools, when to use them, and how they complement your SDK-based agent systems.

Quick Comparison

Framework	Best For	Agent SDK Compatibility
LangChain	Tool use, RAG pipelines, agent memory	Yes (tools, prompts)

Framework	Best For	Agent SDK Compatibility
LangGraph	Multi-agent workflows and state transitions	Yes (modular workflows)
AutoGen	Conversational agent collaboration	Yes (dialogue-based logic)
CrewAI	Role-based teamwork between agents	Yes (task assignment + tools)

1. LangChain Integration

LangChain offers utilities for:

Document loaders (for RAG)

Chains (sequences of steps)

Tool invocation

Memory handling

Example: Use OpenAI Agent in a LangChain Tool

python

```
from langchain.agents import initialize_agent, Tool
from langchain.llms import OpenAI


def run_openai_agent(input):
    # Use your SDK-wrapped agent here
    return my_openai_agent.respond(input)
```

```python
tools = [Tool(name="OpenAI Agent",
func=run_openai_agent, description="Handles general
queries")]

agent = initialize_agent(tools, OpenAI(),
agent="zero-shot-react-description")


agent.run("Summarize the latest customer reviews.")
```

2. LangGraph Integration

LangGraph helps you build graph-based workflows of agents and tools.

Use Case:

Break a task into a sequence like: plan → research → write → review

Example Flow Setup

python

```python
from langgraph.graph import StateGraph


workflow = StateGraph()
workflow.add_node("planner", planner_fn)
workflow.add_node("researcher", research_fn)
workflow.add_node("writer", writer_fn)
workflow.set_entry_point("planner")
workflow.add_edge("planner", "researcher")
workflow.add_edge("researcher", "writer")


graph = workflow.compile()
```

```
graph.invoke("Build a competitive analysis
report.")
```

How it connects: Each node can internally call your OpenAI Agent SDK agent or tool, making LangGraph a **controller layer** on top of your agent logic.

---

3. AutoGen Integration

AutoGen provides a framework for multiple agents to talk to each other through turn-based conversations.

Use Case:

Have a **research agent** and a **decision agent** discuss a problem to find the best answer.

Example: OpenAI Agent Inside AutoGen

```python
python


from autogen import AssistantAgent, UserProxyAgent


researcher = AssistantAgent(name="Researcher",
llm_config={"config_list": openai_config})
decision_maker =
AssistantAgent(name="DecisionMaker",
llm_config={"config_list": openai_config})


user = UserProxyAgent(name="User")


user.initiate_chat(

    recipients=[researcher, decision_maker],

    message="Should we launch the product in Q3?"
```

)

Integration point: You can customize each `AssistantAgent` to use your **OpenAI SDK-wrapped agent** internally or plug it into their `chat` logic.

---

4. CrewAI Integration

CrewAI lets you define a "crew" of agents with roles, goals, and tools.

Example: Role-based Collaboration

python

```
from crewai import Crew, Agent, Task


research_agent = Agent(role="Market Analyst",
goal="Research fintech trends",
tools=[web_search_tool])

writer_agent = Agent(role="Content Writer",
goal="Write article based on research")


task = Task(description="Produce a 500-word blog
post about 2025 fintech trends")


crew = Crew(agents=[research_agent, writer_agent],
tasks=[task])

crew.kickoff()
```

Integration point: Each `Agent` in CrewAI can call your custom OpenAI Agent SDK logic inside their toolchain or during task execution.

When to Use Which

Scenario	Use This Framework
You want custom workflows or pipelines	**LangChain**
You need state-aware, modular task flows	**LangGraph**
You want agent conversations with feedback loops	**AutoGen**
You want to simulate human-like teams	**CrewAI**

Best Practices

Start with OpenAI Agent SDK for core logic.

Wrap the agent in tool functions for LangChain and CrewAI.

For multi-step workflows, use LangGraph.

For dialogue-based collaboration, use AutoGen.

Always use **consistent memory and state** across agents in the swarm.

Summary

Each of these tools enhances the OpenAI Agents SDK in unique ways—LangChain for chaining and tools, LangGraph for workflows, AutoGen for interaction, and CrewAI for structured teams. By combining these with your SDK agents, you can build scalable, collaborative, and production-grade AI systems with ease.

11.6 Exploring the Future of Autonomous AI Agents

The development of autonomous agents is still in its early days—yet they are already reshaping industries, workflows, and human-computer interaction. In this final section, we look at the **emerging trends, technological breakthroughs**, and **future possibilities** that will define the next generation of AI agents built with frameworks like the **OpenAI Agents SDK** and beyond.

1. Next-Gen Capabilities of Autonomous Agents

Capability	Description
Self-Improvement	Agents learn from usage, feedback, and outcomes
Multi-Modality	Seamless reasoning across text, images, audio, and code
Goal-Driven Autonomy	Operate on high-level goals (e.g., "grow my newsletter") and self-plan
Swarm Collaboration	Large groups of agents coordinate like organizations or social networks
Long-Term Memory	Persistent knowledge across sessions and contexts

2. Agents as Teammates, Not Tools

In the near future, agents won't just **answer questions** or **run tasks**—they'll function as:

Project managers for engineering and marketing teams

Operations assistants that monitor and react to real-time changes

Personal strategy advisors that remember your preferences, goals, and constraints

Creative collaborators generating and refining ideas with you

We'll move from "prompt + response" to **ongoing collaboration**.

3. Evolving Architectures

A. Agentic Operating Systems

Layered systems where agents manage tools, memory, and decision-making

Examples: ReAct agents, AutoGPT-style architectures, LangGraph workflows

B. Cognitive Architectures

Combine memory, planning, reflection, and reasoning modules

Inspired by human cognition (e.g., ACT-R, Soar, MemGPT)

C. Decentralized Multi-Agent Networks

Agents with different owners coordinate or compete (e.g., in marketplaces or simulations)

---

4. Challenges That Must Be Solved

Challenge	Why It Matters
Safety and Alignment	Agents must not act unpredictably or outside their boundaries
Transparency and Trust	Users should understand how agents make decisions
Regulatory Compliance	Especially in finance, healthcare, and education
Scalability	Orchestrating 10s–100s of agents in real time
Data Privacy	Maintaining user confidentiality in autonomous interactions

---

5. Trends to Watch

Trend	What to Expect
Agents-as-a-Service (AaaS)	APIs that give you plug-and-play autonomous agents
Regulation-aware agents	Built-in awareness of legal boundaries and policies

Trend	What to Expect
Edge Agents	Agents deployed on local devices for privacy + offline use
Voice + Vision Agents	Multimodal input/output becomes default (GPT-4o, Claude 3)
Open-source agent stacks	Mistral + CrewAI + LangGraph agents in enterprise systems

6. How to Prepare as a Developer

To stay ahead, focus on:

Mastering orchestration frameworks: LangChain, LangGraph, CrewAI, AutoGen

Experimenting with tool use and APIs

Studying multi-agent coordination patterns

Implementing safe, explainable agent designs

Understanding legal and ethical implications

7. Final Vision

The future belongs to developers who can **orchestrate intelligent behavior**, not just call a language model.

You're not building chatbots—you're building:

Autonomous researchers

AI-native departments

Software-driven collaborators

Self-improving digital experts

Summary

337

Autonomous agents are rapidly evolving into **intelligent systems** capable of collaboration, reasoning, learning, and acting in the real world. By staying current with emerging frameworks, tools, and ethical considerations, you'll be ready to shape the future—not just react to it.

In the next and final chapter, we'll wrap up with key takeaways, best practices, and a roadmap for continuing your journey in building real-world autonomous AI systems.

Chapter 12: Troubleshooting and Common Challenges

Even well-designed autonomous agents can fail in unexpected ways. Whether it's hallucinating facts, looping endlessly, or crashing on integration, building production-grade agents requires robust debugging and a good understanding of edge cases.

This chapter provides a **troubleshooting guide**, covering common issues, root causes, and how to fix them when working with the **OpenAI Agents SDK** and related tools.

12.1 Identifying Common Issues

Before you can fix a problem in your agent system, you need to recognize **what's actually going wrong**. This section outlines the most **frequent issues** developers encounter when working with the **OpenAI Agents SDK**, including how to **spot early warning signs**, **diagnose the root cause**, and **prioritize fixes**.

---

1. Categorizing Agent Problems

Start by identifying which layer the issue lives in:

Layer	Typical Issues
Prompt/Model	Hallucination, irrelevant output, inconsistency
Memory/Context	Repetition, forgetfulness, lack of personalization
Tools/API calls	Errors, timeouts, wrong data format
Workflow/Logic	Infinite loops, skipped steps, wrong order
Integration	Slack, database, email, or API failure
Performance/Cost	Slow responses, token overuse, rate limits

---

2. Common Behavioral Symptoms and Root Causes

Symptom	Likely Cause
Agent "makes things up" (hallucinates)	Weak prompt, no grounding, missing RAG
Agent forgets earlier messages	Context window overflow, memory misconfigured
Agent repeats answers or gets stuck	Workflow lacks completion condition or memory loop
Tools aren't triggered as expected	Wrong tool schema, low function confidence
Output has broken formatting (e.g., JSON)	Prompt doesn't enforce strict structure
Long response times	Too many tool/API calls, unoptimized prompt
Crashes on unknown input	No fallback logic or input validation

3. Logging: Your First Debugging Weapon

Add **detailed logs** to trace agent behavior at each step:

Input prompt and metadata

Retrieved documents (if using RAG)

Tool call payload and output

Final response + any exceptions

Example: Basic Logging Snippet

```
python
```

```
import logging
```

```
logging.basicConfig(level=logging.INFO)


def log_agent_step(step, data):

    logging.info(f"[{step}] — {data}")
```

---

4. Quick Diagnostic Checklist

Is the prompt well-scoped and clear?
Are you passing memory or relevant history correctly?
Do tool inputs/outputs match expected schemas?
Are retries or backoffs in place for failed API calls?
Have you tested each agent component independently?
Is the failure repeatable or random?

---

5. Tool: Structured Issue Template

When filing or fixing a bug, use a consistent format:

```
markdown


**Issue Title:** Agent fails to call scheduling API


**Observed Behavior:**

Agent outputs generic response and skips scheduling
tool.


**Expected Behavior:**

Agent should call `schedule_event()` and return
calendar link.


**Environment:**
```

```
OpenAI SDK + LangChain + FastAPI + GPT-4 Turbo
```

Steps to Reproduce:

1. Ask agent to book a meeting for tomorrow.

2. Agent gives vague response, no action triggered.

Suspected Cause:

Tool function not registered or not recognized in prompt.

Suggested Fix:

Check tool decorator + function schema in agent config.

---

6. Prioritization Framework

Use this table to decide what to fix first:

Impact Level	Examples	Priority
High	API crash, security failure, user data loss	Urgent
Medium	Inaccurate output, slow response, tool misuse	High
Low	Minor formatting bugs, tone inconsistency	Normal

Summary

Troubleshooting starts with **spotting the pattern**. Whether your agent forgets things, breaks workflows, or misuses tools, you'll need to trace the error to its layer—prompting, tools, memory, or logic. Logging, reproducible test cases, and structured issue triage will help you fix problems fast and build more stable autonomous systems.

Next, we'll dive deeper into **tool-related failures**, and how to catch and handle them gracefully.

12.2 Debugging Tools and Techniques

Debugging autonomous agents requires more than just checking logs—it means inspecting prompts, tracing decisions, verifying tool calls, and validating memory usage. This section walks you through **practical debugging methods**, along with the **tools and workflows** that experienced developers use to troubleshoot OpenAI Agent SDK-based systems efficiently.

1. Log Everything (Intelligently)

Logging is your first line of defense.

What to Log:

Component	Example
Input Prompt	Final assembled system/user prompt string
Tool Call	Name, input payload, and output
Memory Access	Data retrieved, stored, or summarized
Model Output	Raw LLM response before formatting
Errors	Full traceback or error message

Example: Custom Logging Function

python

```
import logging

logging.basicConfig(level=logging.INFO)


def log_agent_event(event, data):
```

```
logging.info(f"[{event}] → {data}")
```

💡 Tip: Use structured logs (JSON format) for better analysis and searchability.

---

2. Use Streaming Output to Trace LLM Thinking

Enable streaming mode when using `ChatCompletion.create()` to see how the model is reasoning step-by-step.

python

```python
response = openai.ChatCompletion.create(
    model="gpt-4",
    messages=messages,
    stream=True
)


for chunk in response:
    print(chunk.choices[0].delta.get("content",
""), end="", flush=True)
```

This helps debug **where the model gets stuck or changes topic.**

---

3. Prompt Inspection and Replay

Sometimes, the root cause is prompt design. Use a "prompt debugger" pattern to capture and replay prompts.

A. Save and Reload Prompts

python

```python
with open("last_prompt.txt", "w") as f:
```

```
f.write(full_prompt)


# Later

with open("last_prompt.txt", "r") as f:

    replay_prompt = f.read()
```

B. Manually Test in Playground

Copy your prompt into the OpenAI Playground with the same model/settings to reproduce and experiment quickly.

---

4. Trace Tool and Function Failures

Common Issues:

Schema mismatch

Tool not called when expected

Incorrect function output format

Tip: Wrap every tool in a try/except block:

python

```
@tool

def safe_call_api(input: str):

    try:

        result = external_api_call(input)

        return result

    except Exception as e:

        log_agent_event("ToolError", str(e))

        return "Tool failed due to an error."
```

Also test tools independently before wiring into the agent.

5. Visualize Workflows and State (LangGraph + CrewAI)

If you're using **LangGraph** or **CrewAI**, use visual inspection to debug agent flow:

LangGraph Example:

```python
```

```python
graph.get_graph().draw(output_file="workflow.png")
```

This generates a visual diagram of nodes, paths, and transitions—ideal for spotting logic errors or missing edges.

---

6. Use Evaluation Tools (Optional but Powerful)

Tool	Use Case
LangSmith	Track traces, prompt versions, metrics
OpenAI Evals	Run structured tests on model behavior
PromptLayer	Log, version, and compare prompt performance

You can even define expected inputs/outputs and run unit tests against them.

---

7. Test with Known Inputs

Create a set of test prompts and expected responses:

```python
```

```python
tests = [
  {"input": "Summarize this article", "context":
"...", "expect": "Short summary"},
```

```
    {"input": "Schedule a meeting", "expect_tool":
"schedule_event"}
]
```

```
for test in tests:
    result = agent.run(test["input"])
    assert test["expect"] in result
```

This ensures updates don't break core agent functionality.

8. Monitor API Usage and Errors

Track:

Token usage per call (usage object in OpenAI response)

API error types (e.g., RateLimitError, InvalidRequestError)

Function call frequency

Sample Error Catching:

python

```
try:
    response = openai.ChatCompletion.create(...)
except openai.error.RateLimitError:
    time.sleep(5)
    retry()
```

Summary

Debugging autonomous agents is part science, part strategy. With solid logging, prompt replay, streaming inspection, and structured testing, you can quickly diagnose and fix problems in your agent workflows. As complexity grows, rely on tools like LangGraph, LangSmith, and PromptLayer to gain deep visibility and stay in control.

12.3 Managing Unexpected Agent Behaviors

Even with solid prompts and workflows, **autonomous agents can behave in unpredictable ways**—generating irrelevant answers, taking inappropriate actions, or drifting off-task. These behaviors are common, especially in dynamic environments or when agents are granted tool access and memory. This section shows how to **anticipate, detect, and manage** these behaviors with guardrails, monitoring, and recovery strategies.

1. Common Types of Unexpected Behaviors

Behavior Type	Example
Hallucination	Agent fabricates facts or unsupported claims
Instruction Drift	Agent starts doing something unrelated to the original task
Overconfidence	Agent gives firm answers without enough evidence or certainty
Tool misuse	Agent calls the wrong tool or calls a tool with invalid parameters
Infinite loops or repeats	Agent gets stuck repeating the same step or message
Unstructured output	Returns incomplete, malformed, or inconsistent formats (e.g., bad JSON)

2. Prevention Through Prompt Design

Use Role + Task Clarity

python

```
"You are a strict assistant that ONLY answers
questions related to company policy."
```

Include Do/Don't Instructions

python

```
"DO: Provide clear, factual answers.\nDON'T: Assume
or invent information not present in the context."
```

Provide Format Expectations

python

```
"Return your answer as a JSON object with 'answer'
and 'source' fields only."
```

Consistent instructions help anchor the model's behavior within boundaries.

---

3. Add Confidence Scoring and Escalation Logic

Let your agent **self-assess uncertainty** or use heuristics to flag low-confidence output.

Example Heuristic:

python

```python
def should_escalate(response: str) -> bool:
    low_confidence_phrases = ["I think", "I'm not
sure", "It might be"]

    return any(phrase in response.lower() for
phrase in low_confidence_phrases)
```

If triggered, redirect to a fallback, human review, or clarification prompt.

---

4. Set Output Validators and Format Checkers

Example: JSON Format Validator

python

```
import json

def is_valid_json(output: str) -> bool:
    try:
        json.loads(output)
        return True
    except json.JSONDecodeError:
        return False
```

If invalid, re-prompt the model with a correction:

python

```
"Please reformat your previous response as valid
JSON only. No additional text."
```

---

5. Handle Infinite Loops and Repeats

Problem: Agent keeps asking follow-up questions or repeating steps.

Fixes:

Set a max number of steps (`max_iterations`)

Store previous steps in memory and check for repetition

Use LangGraph with explicit state transitions and stop conditions

python

```
if iteration_count > 5:

    log_event("Loop detected. Terminating.")

    return "Agent reached max steps."
```

6. Use Guardrails and Output Moderation

Guardrail Strategies:

Strategy	Use Case
Output regex check	Validate output format before accepting
Content filters	Block unsafe or inappropriate responses
Fallback instructions	Retry with a safer prompt version
Access control wrappers	Limit tool usage based on context

Tool: Guardrails AI

Enforce structure, content boundaries, and failover logic

Works with OpenAI, LangChain, and custom models

7. Logging and Replay for Behavior Audits

Unexpected agent decisions should be logged for human review:

python

```
log = {
  "input": user_input,
  "context": context_used,
  "output": agent_response,
  "tools_called": called_tools,
  "confidence_flag": flagged_as_low
```

}

Store these logs for weekly audits or to fine-tune future prompts/models.

---

8. Auto-Correction Strategies

If output fails a test (format, accuracy, etc.), automatically re-prompt the agent:

python

```
if not is_valid_json(output):

    correction_prompt = f"""

    The previous output was not valid JSON.
Reformat strictly as:

    {{

      "answer": "...",

      "source": "..."

    }}

    """

    corrected_output = agent.run(correction_prompt)
```

Summary

Unexpected behaviors are a natural part of autonomous agent systems—but with structured prompts, guardrails, confidence checks, validators, and escalation logic, you can **detect, control, and recover from these behaviors** reliably.

In the next section, we'll cover how to **handle integration-level failures**, such as broken API calls, database errors, or external system timeouts.

12.4 Resolving Performance Bottlenecks

Autonomous agents are powerful—but they can be **slow, expensive, or inefficient** if not designed and optimized carefully. This section focuses on how to **identify, diagnose, and fix performance bottlenecks** when building agents with the **OpenAI Agents SDK**, especially in production environments where latency, cost, and responsiveness matter.

1. Common Performance Bottlenecks

Bottleneck Type	Symptoms
Prompt Overhead	Large prompts = slow generation, high token cost
Tool/Function Delays	API latency, retry loops, or long-running functions
Context Overflow	Unnecessary memory/context slows response times
High Token Usage	Prompt + history too large, repeating data
Redundant Reasoning	Agent rethinks known steps or repeats logic
Workflow Inefficiency	Unnecessary state transitions or extra tool invocations

2. Measure First: Performance Metrics to Track

Metric	How to Track
Response time (latency)	Time per agent run (e.g. `time.perf_counter()`)
Token usage	`response['usage']['total_tokens']`
Tool duration	Log timestamps before and after tool calls

Metric	How to Track
Step count	Number of loops or actions taken

Use structured logs to measure and compare over time.

---

3. Optimize Prompts for Speed and Cost

Problem: Long, bloated prompts slow the model and inflate costs.

Fixes:

Avoid repeating context or instructions unnecessarily

Use short summaries of prior conversation/memory

Switch to GPT-4 Turbo (cheaper, more context) or GPT-3.5 for simpler tasks

Example: Concise Prompt Template

```python
"You are a support agent. Answer based on the facts
below."


Facts: {retrieved_docs}


User: {query}
```

Keep instructions under 100 tokens if possible.

---

4. Use Caching for Repeated Queries

If your agent answers repeated or deterministic queries:

```python
from functools import lru_cache
```

```
@lru_cache(maxsize=128)

def get_response(prompt):

    return agent.run(prompt)
```

Or use Redis/SQLite for persistent cache between sessions.

---

5. Optimize Tool and API Calls

Optimization Strategy	Result
Add timeouts and retries	Prevent hanging or failing calls
Batch or bulk fetch when possible	Reduce overhead and improve throughput
Memoize or cache static results	Avoid repeat API hits for the same data
Use lightweight services	Prefer internal endpoints over 3rd-party APIs

Example: Set timeout

```
python
```

```
requests.get(url, timeout=5)
```

---

6. Reduce Context Window Usage

Agents slow down when pushing against the model's context limit (especially GPT-4).

Fixes:

Trim history to essentials (`last user input`, `last agent reply`)

Summarize older conversations

Store persistent memory externally (e.g., Redis or PostgreSQL)

Example: Context Summarization

python

```
"Earlier we discussed refund policies and ticket
#12345."
```

This preserves continuity without bloating tokens.

---

7. Use Model Selection Strategically

Task Type	Recommended Model
Complex reasoning	`gpt-4-turbo`
Simple Q&A or lookups	`gpt-3.5-turbo`
High-volume tool routing	`gpt-3.5-turbo-1106`

Strategy: Route non-critical subtasks to faster/cheaper models.

---

8. Parallelize Multi-Agent Workflows

If using multiple agents:

Run agents in **parallel** for independent subtasks (e.g. research, analysis)

Use **async/await** or Python multiprocessing

python

```python
import asyncio

async def run_agents():
    result1, result2 = await
asyncio.gather(agent1.run(), agent2.run())
```

---

9. Profile Your System

Use tools like:

`cProfile` or `line_profiler` (Python)

LangSmith traces (LangChain)

Time logs in custom observability dashboards

Track:

Longest-running steps

Tool/API bottlenecks

Slow model responses

---

10. Build a Performance Baseline

Create a simple test suite with:

Average latency per task

Token usage per response

Tool response time

Agent step count

Use this baseline to compare after each update or optimization.

Summary

Performance optimization isn't just about speed—it's about **scaling efficiently and cost-effectively**. By shortening prompts, caching responses, limiting context, refining tool usage, and measuring consistently, you can deploy OpenAI agents that feel fast, responsive, and affordable at scale.

In the next and final section, we'll close out with a checklist and guide to building production-ready agents with confidence.

12.5 FAQs and Quick Solutions Guide

This section serves as your **fast-access cheat sheet** for resolving the most frequently encountered issues when working with the **OpenAI Agents SDK**. Whether you're debugging behavior, fixing output formatting, or optimizing costs, use this FAQ to find **quick answers and actionable fixes**.

GENERAL USAGE

Q1: My agent is returning generic or irrelevant answers. What should I do?

Quick Fixes:

Refine the **system prompt** to be role-specific and clear.

Add examples (few-shot prompting).

Use **RAG** to include relevant knowledge.

Q2: The agent forgets earlier interactions. Why?

Causes:

Token context limit reached.

Memory not configured or retrieved properly.

Solutions:

Use summarization for long conversations.

Externalize memory with a database or Redis.

Trim memory context to only recent or essential steps.

Q3: How do I get structured outputs (like JSON) reliably?

Best Practices:

Add format constraints in the prompt:

"Respond with a valid JSON object using the fields: title, body, and status."

Use `response_format="json"` (if supported by SDK).

Validate output before using it (with `json.loads()`).

⬚⬚ TOOLS AND FUNCTION CALLING

Q4: Why isn't my tool/function being triggered?

Likely Causes:

Function definition isn't registered properly.

LLM doesn't understand when/how to call it.

Fixes:

Set `function_call="auto"` or `function_call={"name": "your_function_name"}`.

Include usage examples in the system prompt.

Make sure function parameters are defined correctly.

Q5: Tools are returning errors or not working.

Checklist:

Add error handling inside your tool functions.

Log all inputs and outputs for visibility.

Test the tool independently before wiring into agent logic.

PERFORMANCE & COST

Q6: My agent is too slow. How can I speed it up?

Quick Solutions:

Shorten prompts and reduce memory/context size.

Switch to faster models for simpler tasks (e.g., GPT-3.5).

Cache repeated tool calls or agent responses.

Use async execution for multi-agent flows.

Q7: I'm hitting rate limits. What can I do?

Fixes:

Add exponential backoff in retry logic.

Use `openai.error.RateLimitError` handler.

Apply batching or throttle requests per second.

MEMORY AND CONTEXT

Q8: My agent is repeating itself or stuck in a loop.

Solutions:

Set a `max_iterations` limit.

Track state transitions (use LangGraph or a step counter).

Compare current prompt with last one—terminate on duplication.

Q9: Agent is "hallucinating" or making things up.

Best Practices:

Use RAG to ground responses with external data.

Include disclaimers in the prompt like:

"Only answer if you are sure, otherwise say 'I don't know.'"

Add output validators or confidence thresholds.

DEPLOYMENT & INTEGRATION

Q10: Agent can't connect to APIs or databases.

Fixes:

Double-check API keys and environment variables.

Add timeout and retry logic to external calls.

Use secure secret storage (`dotenv`, AWS Secrets Manager, etc.).

Q11: My Slack/Email/Calendar integration isn't working.

Checklist:

Validate credentials (OAuth, webhook URL).

Use correct API endpoints and formats.

Test each integration outside of the agent before combining.

STRUCTURED TROUBLESHOOTING TEMPLATE

Use this for debugging any issue:

```markdown


**Issue Title:** Agent repeats last step in locp


**Behavior:** Agent keeps replying "Let me check
that again."


**Suspected Cause:** No memory validation or locp
breaker


**Fix Attempted:** Added `max_iterations=3` and
checked memory logs
```

Next Steps: Introduce step tracker and stop if same response repeats

---

☐ Recommended Tools for Debugging

Tool	Purpose
LangSmith	Tracing, logging, agent step visualization
PromptLayer	Prompt version control and monitoring
Guardrails AI	Enforce structured output and validations
LangGraph Debug	Visual workflow testing

Summary

Use this FAQ whenever you're stuck—whether it's broken tool calls, fuzzy responses, or slow agents. Combined with good logging, testing, and structure, these quick-fix patterns will help you resolve most issues **without interrupting development flow**.

Bookmark this section as your **first stop when things break.**

In the final chapter, we'll wrap up everything you've learned and provide a roadmap for scaling your agent systems from prototype to production.

Chapter 13: Conclusion and Next Steps

Final Thoughts

Congratulations! You've reached the end of **OpenAI Agents SDK: A Hands-On Guide to Building Autonomous Agents with OpenAI's Language Models**. By now, you've explored everything from the core architecture and setup to advanced multi-agent orchestration, predictive reasoning, and production deployment.

Autonomous AI agents aren't just a trend—they're a powerful evolution in how software interacts with the world. You now have the tools to build agents that can **think, decide, act, and improve**—not just answer questions.

13.1 Summary of Key Learnings

Throughout this book, you've gained a **complete, hands-on understanding** of how to build, manage, and scale autonomous AI agents using the **OpenAI Agents SDK**—from the basics of setup to advanced multi-agent systems and real-world applications.

Let's recap the most important concepts and skills you've learned.

Foundations and Setup

How to install and configure the **OpenAI Agents SDK** locally and in the cloud.

How to securely manage **API keys**, environment variables, and secrets.

How to build your **first working agent** with minimal code.

Core Concepts

The **anatomy of an agent**: prompts, memory, tools, function calling, context.

Understanding the **agent lifecycle**—from initialization to termination.

Selecting and integrating the right **language models** (GPT-4 Turbo, GPT-4o).

Applying **prompt engineering techniques** for clarity, structure, and reliability.

Agent Development

Building **single-agent workflows** for focused, useful tasks.

Creating **multi-agent collaborations** with LangGraph and CrewAI.

Handling **tool use, APIs, RAG**, and database integrations.

Building real-world agents like:

Task schedulers

Customer support bots

Marketing content generators

Autonomous research assistants

Advanced Capabilities

Fine-tuning models for **domain-specific behavior**.

Using **RAG** to reduce hallucinations and improve accuracy.

Designing agents that can **predict, reason, and make decisions**.

Constructing **multi-modal agents** that handle text, voice, vision, and structured data.

Debugging and Optimization

How to **log, trace, and fix** common errors.

Techniques for **debugging prompts**, tool usage, loops, and output formats.

Improving agent **speed, cost-efficiency, and reliability** with smart patterns.

Security, Ethics, and Production Readiness

Strategies for ensuring **data privacy**, compliance (e.g., GDPR), and responsible AI use.

Guarding against bias, abuse, and misbehavior.

Deploying agents safely into **production environments** with observabil_ty and fallback logic.

Real-World Use Cases

You explored how agents are being used across industries like:

Industry	Use Case Examples
Finance	Investment advisors, portfolio summaries
Healthcare	Patient intake agents, data triage
Marketing	Content generation, campaign planners
Enterprise	Knowledge assistants, workflow automation
Research	Literature reviews, data summarization

Integration with the Ecosystem

Connected OpenAI agents to **LangChain** for chaining and tool use.

Used **LangGraph** for task flow logic and state management.

Enabled **AutoGen** for collaborative multi-agent dialogue.

Deployed with **CrewAI** for role-based agent teams.

Future Outlook

Agents will evolve into **autonomous digital teammates**.

Emerging trends include **swarm systems**, **goal-driven agents**, **continual learning**, and **regulatory-aware automation**.

You're equipped to lead, experiment, and scale in the **next era of AI development**.

You've done more than just learn the SDK—you've built a solid foundation for **agentic thinking** and real-world AI engineering.

Whether you're solving internal workflow problems or building products for users, the principles and tools you've mastered in this book will continue to serve you in every project ahead.

This isn't the end—it's your launchpad.
You now have everything you need to create, deploy, and scale the agents of the future.

13.2 Continuous Learning Resources and Next Steps
Mastering the **OpenAI Agents SDK** is just the beginning. The world of autonomous agents is evolving rapidly—with new tools, frameworks, and best practices emerging every month.

This section gives you a **handpicked list of learning resources**, practical ways to keep building, and a clear roadmap to help you **grow from builder to expert** in the agent development space.

Curated Learning Resources

OpenAI Official Resources

OpenAI Agents SDK Docs
https://platform.openai.com/docs/agents

Function Calling & Tool Use
https://platform.openai.com/docs/guides/function-calling

Fine-Tuning Guide
https://platform.openai.com/docs/guides/fine-tuning

Agent Ecosystem Docs

LangChain Docs (for RAG and chaining)
https://docs.langchain.com

LangGraph (for workflow coordination)
https://github.com/langchain-ai/langgraph

AutoGen by Microsoft
https://github.com/microsoft/autogen

CrewAI (for multi-agent collaboration)
https://github.com/joaomdmoura/crewai

Testing & Monitoring Tools

LangSmith – for tracing, debugging, and evaluating agent flows
https://smith.langchain.com

PromptLayer – prompt version control and monitoring
https://promptlayer.com

Guardrails AI – enforce structure, safety, and reliability
https://github.com/guardrails-ai/guardrails

Your Agent Development Roadmap

Stage	Action Item
Level 1	Build simple task agents with OpenAI SDK
Level 2	Add memory, tools, and structured outputs
Level 3	Deploy agents with RAG, tools, and API integrations
Level 4	Design multi-agent systems (LangGraph, CrewAI)
Level 5	Fine-tune models, optimize cost, monitor in prod
Level 6	Lead AI projects, mentor others, open-source tools

Next Project Ideas

AI Meeting Summarizer → Slack + Calendar + Notes Agent

Financial Research Agent → RAG + PDF reader + chart generator

Internal Knowledge Agent → LangChain + FAISS + OpenAI + Audit Logging

Product Feedback Agent → Collect, analyze, and summarize user reviews

Onboarding Agent → Personalized HR assistant for new employees

---

Join the Community

Stay up-to-date and learn from other builders:

OpenAI Community Forum

LangChain Discord

CrewAI GitHub Discussions

AI Engineer's YouTube and Twitter

Final Steps to Mastery

Keep shipping → Build small projects weekly

Stay curious → Test new features and releases

Contribute back → Share what you build with others

Refactor often → Treat agents like production systems

Document everything → Prompts, tools, memory, workflows

You've now got the **knowledge, structure, and skill** to build powerful autonomous agents. But the most important thing you can do next is simple:

Keep going. Build more. Learn by doing. Share your work.
This is how real mastery begins.

Let the world see what your agents can do. The future is waiting—go lead it.

13.3 Staying Updated with Industry Trends

The agent ecosystem—especially around the **OpenAI Agents SDK**—is evolving fast. New features, frameworks, and best practices are released almost weekly. To remain competitive and keep building cutting-edge systems, you need to stay connected to **industry trends**, **tooling updates**, and **real-world use cases**.

This section offers a strategy to help you **track the pulse of the industry**, so you can continuously learn, adapt, and lead.

Follow High-Signal Sources

Platform	What to Watch For
OpenAI Changelog	SDK updates, model releases, new capabilities
LangChain Weekly	Feature drops, integrations, best practices
GitHub Repos	AutoGen, LangGraph, CrewAI – watch and follow
Papers with Code	Latest research in autonomous agents and AI tools
AI Twitter (X)	Follow top devs like @amasad, @swyx, @andrewyng
YouTube Channels	"AI Explained", "AssemblyAI", "Fireship", "AI Engineer"

Join Communities and Events

Developer Forums & Discords

OpenAI Developer Forum

369

LangChain Discord

CrewAI GitHub Discussions

[AI Town, SuperAGI, and AutoGen channels on Discord and Slack]

Conferences & Webinars

OpenAI Dev Day (annual)

Hugging Face & LangChain meetups

AI Engineering Summits (e.g., by Latent Space or Weights & Biases)

Watch These Trends Closely

Trend	Why It Matters
Agent OS & Orchestration	LangGraph, CrewAI, AutoGen – core to managing complexity
RAG + Tool Fusion	Combining retrieval and tool use into seamless pipelines
Multimodal Agents	GPT-4o and beyond—text, vision, voice, video
Swarm Architectures	Dozens of agents working in coordinated, autonomous groups
Custom Models + Fine-Tuning	Domain-specific intelligence for competitive differentiation
Real-Time Agents	Agents that react live—via voice, sensors, or chat input
Ethical & Regulatory AI	Compliance, bias mitigation, and safety guardrails

---

Tools to Stay Ahead

Tool	Use Case
LangSmith	Trace, debug, and improve agents
PromptLayer	Track and version your prompt changes
Guardrails AI	Enforce structured, safe agent behavior
AgentOps (Coming)	Manage deployment, monitoring, and scaling

Pro Tips

Set a monthly review routine: Check changelogs and GitHub discussions.

Watch key repo issues/PRs: Stay ahead of SDK improvements and edge cases.

Bookmark live dashboards: SDKs like LangGraph and CrewAI often have live demos.

Run weekly experiments: Try new tools, models, or workflows in a sandbox project.

Final Thought

Staying updated isn't just about consuming content—it's about **experimenting with new tools, sharing your findings, and engaging with the builder community**. That's how the best AI developers stay ahead of the curve.

The agent world is moving fast—but you're now equipped to move faster.

13.3 Staying Updated with Industry Trends

The agent ecosystem—especially around the **OpenAI Agents SDK**—is evolving fast. New features, frameworks, and best practices are released almost weekly. To remain competitive and keep building cutting-edge systems, you need to stay connected to **industry trends**, **tooling updates**, and **real-world use cases**.

This section offers a strategy to help you **track the pulse of the industry**, so you can continuously learn, adapt, and lead.

Follow High-Signal Sources

Platform	What to Watch For
OpenAI Changelog	SDK updates, model releases, new capabilities
LangChain Weekly	Feature drops, integrations, best practices
GitHub Repos	AutoGen, LangGraph, CrewAI – watch and follow
Papers with Code	Latest research in autonomous agents and AI tools
AI Twitter (X)	Follow top devs like @amasad, @swyx, @andrewyng
YouTube Channels	"AI Explained", "AssemblyAI", "Fireship", "AI Engineer"

Join Communities and Events

Developer Forums & Discords

OpenAI Developer Forum

LangChain Discord

CrewAI GitHub Discussions

[AI Town, SuperAGI, and AutoGen channels on Discord and Slack]

Conferences & Webinars

OpenAI Dev Day (annual)

Hugging Face & LangChain meetups

AI Engineering Summits (e.g., by Latent Space or Weights & Biases)

☐ Watch These Trends Closely

Trend	Why It Matters
Agent OS & Orchestration	LangGraph, CrewAI, AutoGen – core to managing complexity
RAG + Tool Fusion	Combining retrieval and tool use into seamless pipelines
Multimodal Agents	GPT-4o and beyond—text, vision, voice, video
Swarm Architectures	Dozens of agents working in coordinated, autonomous groups
Custom Models + Fine-Tuning	Domain-specific intelligence for competitive differentiation
Real-Time Agents	Agents that react live—via voice, sensors, or chat input
Ethical & Regulatory AI	Compliance, bias mitigation, and safety guardrails

Tools to Stay Ahead

Tool	Use Case
LangSmith	Trace, debug, and improve agents
PromptLayer	Track and version your prompt changes
Guardrails AI	Enforce structured, safe agent behavior
AgentOps (Coming)	Manage deployment, monitoring, and scaling

Pro Tips

Set a monthly review routine: Check changelogs and GitHub discussions.

Watch key repo issues/PRs: Stay ahead of SDK improvements and edge cases.

Bookmark live dashboards: SDKs like LangGraph and CrewAI often have live demos.

Run weekly experiments: Try new tools, models, or workflows in a sandbox project.

Staying updated isn't just about consuming content—it's about **experimenting with new tools, sharing your findings, and engaging with the builder community**. That's how the best AI developers stay ahead of the curve.

The agent world is moving fast—but you're now equipped to move faster.

Keep learning, keep building, and keep leading.

13.4 Final Recommendations for Building Successful Agents

As you prepare to build your own real-world agent systems, it's critical to apply **lessons learned** from this book in a structured, reliable way. This final section offers **battle-tested recommendations** for ensuring your agents are not only functional—but **intelligent, safe, scalable, and production-ready**.

---

1. Start Simple, Scale Smart

Don't begin with complex multi-agent swarms. Start with:

A single-agent task (e.g., summarizing, replying, analyzing)

Add tools or RAG only when needed

Once validated, expand into workflows or multi-agent teams

Simplicity first. Structure second. Scale last.

---

2. Be Obsessive About Prompt Clarity

A great agent starts with a great prompt. Always:

Define the role clearly: e.g., "You are a security analyst..."

Set strict output expectations: e.g., "Return only a JSON object..."

Include edge case instructions: e.g., "If unsure, respond with 'I don't know.'"

Maintain a versioned prompt library like you would code.

3. Use Tools Intelligently

Only register **essential tools** per agent.

Keep tool schemas strict and validated.

Always wrap external calls in error handling.

Log tool inputs/outputs for transparency and debugging.

Avoid tool overload. Let each agent do one job well.

4. Leverage RAG for Factual Precision

Use RAG when:

Agents must cite internal knowledge or recent data

You need grounded, source-backed answers

You want to reduce hallucination risk

Always test:

Document quality and chunking

Retrieval relevance

Prompt injection of retrieved content

If accuracy matters, ground it in your data.

5. Design Agents with Modularity

Think of agents as components in a larger system. Design with:

Clearly scoped tasks

Inter-agent messaging patterns (e.g., planner → executor → reviewer)

Separation of concerns (don't mix memory, tools, and logic in one blob)

Reuse agents across multiple workflows.

---

6. Build With Safety from Day One

Include in every project:

Content filters (for output moderation)

JSON schema validators (for output structure)

Max iterations and fallback logic (for loops and failures)

Logging and audit trails (for compliance and traceability)

Secure agents are trusted agents.

---

7. Focus on Production Readiness Early

Before deploying agents live:

Optimize for **latency and token cost**

Build **observability dashboards** (LangSmith, Prometheus, logs)

Add **monitoring and alerts** for tool/API failures

Containerize with **Docker** and deploy to scalable platforms (Kubernetes, serverless)

Production isn't the end—it's the beginning of iteration.

---

8. Always Test, Measure, and Improve

Create a **test suite** with known queries and expected responses

Track performance metrics: latency, tokens, success rate

Collect user feedback for prompt and logic refinement

Revisit architecture every few months as models/tools evolve

Build → Measure → Learn → Refine → Repeat

Summary

To build truly successful agents:

- **Start small, prompt well, scale modularly**
- **Use RAG for truth, tools for action, memory for flow**
- **Design for debugging, security, and resilience**
- **Deploy with care—and improve continuously**

With these practices, you're not just building agents. You're building **real-world AI systems** that people can rely on.

Intelligent agents aren't made by chance. They're engineered with clarity, structure, and purpose.

You're now ready to go from developer to AI architect. Let's build agents that matter.

Appendices

Appendix A: OpenAI Agents SDK Complete Reference

This appendix provides a detailed of the **key functions, classes, and components** available in the OpenAI Agents SDK. Use it as a technical reference while building or debugging agents in real-world applications.

A.1 SDK Functions and Classes

◆ `openai.Agents.create()`

Purpose: Initializes a new autonomous agent.

python

```
openai.Agents.create(

    name="support_agent",

    instructions="You are a helpful customer
support assistant.",

    model="gpt-4-turbo",

    tools=[...],

    memory=True

)
```

Parameter	Description
name	Unique identifier for the agent
instructions	System prompt defining the agent's role
model	Model to use (e.g., gpt-4, gpt-4-turbo)
tools	List of tools the agent can access
memory	Enables context retention across invocations

◆ openai.Agents.call()

Purpose: Sends input to the agent and returns the agent's response.

python

```
openai.Agents.call(
    agent_id="support_agent",
    input="How do I reset my password?"
)
```

Parameter Description

`agent_id` ID of the agent being called

`input`   User input or question

Returns a structured response including:

Agent reply

Any tool invocations

Metadata and context used

◆ openai.Agents.tools.FunctionTool

Purpose: Defines a tool (function) that agents can invoke.

python

```
from openai.agents.tools import FunctionTool

def check_order_status(order_id: str) -> str:
    # Custom business logic here
```

```
    return f"Order {order_id} is in transit."
```

```
tool =
FunctionTool.from_function(check_order_status)
```

Method	Description
`from_function(func)`	Registers a Python function as a tool
`name`	Tool name used in agent calls
`description`	Description shown to the model
`parameters`	JSON schema inferred from function

◆ `openai.Agents.list()`

Purpose: Lists all registered agents.

`python`

```
openai.Agents.list()
```

◆ `openai.Agents.get(agent_id)`

Purpose: Retrieves a specific agent by ID.

`python`

```
openai.Agents.get("support_agent")
```

◆ `openai.Agents.update(agent_id, **kwargs)`

Purpose: Updates an existing agent's configuration.

`python`

```python
openai.Agents.update("support_agent",
instructions="Updated instructions.")
```

◆ openai.Agents.delete(agent_id)

Purpose: Removes an agent and its configuration.

python

```python
openai.Agents.delete("support_agent")
```

◆ openai.Agents.memory.*

If memory is enabled, you can access memory operations:

Method	Purpose
memory.append(agent_id, data)	Manually store memory
memory.clear(agent_id)	Clears memory for an agent
memory.retrieve(agent_id)	Retrieves stored memory

Tips for Using SDK Functions

Wrap tools with error handling.

Modularize agent creation and calling in your codebase.

Use **UUIDs** or naming conventions to track agent instances.

Store **agent configs in files or databases** for version control.

A.2 SDK Error Codes and Troubleshooting

This section covers common **error codes, exceptions,** and **troubleshooting steps** when working with the **OpenAI Agents SDK.** Use it to diagnose failures quickly and implement graceful recovery strategies in your applications.

Common SDK Error Types

Error Type	Description
`openai.error.InvalidRequestError`	Invalid arguments passed (e.g., bad tool schema, missing input)
`openai.error.AuthenticationError`	API key is missing, expired, or incorrect
`openai.error.PermissionError`	API key does not have permission to use Agents SDK
`openai.error.RateLimitError`	Too many requests sent in a short time window
`openai.error.APIConnectionError`	Network issue or OpenAI server temporarily unreachable
`openai.error.ServiceUnavailableError`	Temporary downtime or high server load
`openai.error.OpenAIError`	Base class for general SDK errors

Typical Error Messages and Fixes

◆ **InvalidRequestError**

Message:
```
Invalid tool definition: expected 'parameters' as
valid JSON schema.
```

Cause:

Your tool function is missing type hints or returns an unsupported data type.

Fix:

Ensure all function parameters and return types are properly annotated.

python

```python
def get_weather(city: str) -> str:  # Good
    ...
```

◆ **AuthenticationError**

Message:
```
No API key provided.
```

Cause:

Missing or misconfigured OPENAI_API_KEY.

Fix:

Set your key using environment variable or SDK config:

bash

```bash
export OPENAI_API_KEY="your-key-here"
```

Or:

python

```python
import openai
```

```
openai.api_key = "your-key-here"
```

◆ PermissionError

Message:
```
You do not have access to the /v1/agents endpoint.
```

Cause:

API key is not part of the beta or does not have Agents access.

Fix:

Apply for API access on OpenAI's platform

Check your usage plan or organization permissions.

◆ RateLimitError

Message:
```
You are sending requests too quickly.
```

Fixes:

Implement retry logic with exponential backoff:

```python
import time

def retry_with_backoff(call_fn, retries=3):
    for i in range(retries):
        try:
            return call_fn()
        except openai.error.RateLimitError:
            time.sleep(2 ** i)
```

Use fewer concurrent calls or upgrade to higher rate limits.

◆ ServiceUnavailableError / APIConnectionError

Message:
`Failed to connect to the OpenAI API.`

Cause:

Temporary server issue or unstable network connection.

Fix:

Retry after a few seconds.

Log failures and alert your team if they persist.

Troubleshooting Checklist

Area	What to Check
Agent creation	Valid `instructions`, `tools`, `model`, and `name`
Tool use	Valid function schema, proper type hints, safe output
Memory issues	Ensure `memory=True` is enabled and supported by model
Output format	Use structured prompts and JSON formatting if needed
Token overuse	Monitor token count using `response['usage']`
Long latency	Minimize prompt size and avoid unnecessary context

---

Logging Tip for All SDK Errors

Use structured exception handling to catch and report all OpenAI-related errors:

```python
python
```

```
import openai


try:

    result = openai.Agents.call(...)

except openai.error.OpenAIError as e:

    print(f"[ERROR] OpenAI SDK failed:
{type(e).__name__} - {str(e)}")
```
Always log both the **error type** and **message** to simplify debugging.

By understanding and catching common SDK errors proactively, you can build agent systems that are **resilient, self-recovering, and production-safe**. In the next appendix, we'll provide a full example walkthrough that ties everything together using the SDK from end to end.

Appendix B: Quickstart Templates and Cheat Sheets
B.1 Agent Project Templates

This section provides **plug-and-play project templates** to help you quickly bootstrap agent-powered applications using the **OpenAI Agents SDK**. These templates include code structure, agent creation logic, and tool wiring— designed to get you from zero to running in minutes.

Template 1: Simple Autonomous Assistant

A minimal agent that responds to user questions.

```python


import openai


# Configure API Key
```

```python
openai.api_key = "your-api-key"


# Create agent
agent = openai.Agents.create(
    name="simple_assistant",
    instructions="You are a helpful, concise
assistant. Respond clearly.",
    model="gpt-4-turbo",
    tools=[],
    memory=True
)


# Call the agent
response = openai.Agents.call(
    agent_id=agent.id,
    input="How do I reset my password?"
)


print(response["output"])
```

Template 2: Agent with Tool Integration

Agent that uses a registered function to fetch data.

```python
from openai.agents.tools import FunctionTool
import openai
```

```python
# Define a tool
def get_order_status(order_id: str) -> str:
    return f"Order {order_id} is in transit."


tool = FunctionTool.from_function(get_order_status)


# Create agent
agent = openai.Agents.create(
    name="order_helper",
    instructions="You help customers check order status.",
    model="gpt-4-turbo",
    tools=[tool],
    memory=False
)


# Call the agent
response = openai.Agents.call(
    agent_id=agent.id,
    input="Check status for order 12345"
)


print(response["output"])
```

Template 3: Agent with Memory + History

python

```
import openai

openai.api_key = "your-api-key"

# Create memory-enabled agent
agent = openai.Agents.create(
    name="history_agent",
    instructions="You are a smart assistant that
remembers past conversations.",
    model="gpt-4-turbo",
    memory=True
)

# Run first call
response_1 = openai.Agents.call(agent_id=agent.id,
input="What is your name?")
print(response_1["output"])

# Run second call
response_2 = openai.Agents.call(agent_id=agent.id,
input="What did I ask you earlier?")
print(response_2["output"])
```

Recommended Project Folder Structure

plaintext

```
agent_project/
├── main.py                  # Entrypoint for your agent
├── tools/
│   └── finance_tools.py     # Custom tools for agent
├── config/
│   └── agent_config.json    # Agent metadata or model config
├── memory/
│   └── memory_store.json    # Optional external memory
└── utils/
    └── logger.py            # Logging and debugging helpers
```

Agent Creation Checklist

Step

API key configured

Agent created with instructions

Model selected (e.g. gpt-4-turbo)

Tools properly registered

Input/output logging enabled

Step

Memory enabled if needed

Try/except around API calls

Testing Agent Calls

python

```
def test_agent(agent_id, test_input,
expected_phrase):
    result = openai.Agents.call(agent_id=agent_id,
input=test_input)
    assert expected_phrase.lower() in
result["output"].lower()
```

Use this to quickly validate your agents are behaving as expected.

Summary

These templates help you spin up new agents in minutes—whether you're building assistants, tool-driven agents, or memory-enabled workflows. Use them as scaffolds for more advanced projects throughout your autonomous agent journey.

B.2 Prompt Engineering Cheat Sheets

Prompt engineering is the core skill that controls **how your agent thinks, responds, and uses tools**. This cheat sheet gives you high-impact templates, patterns, and best practices to help your OpenAI agents behave consistently and intelligently.

◆ **Essential Prompt Structure**

```
text
```

```
You are a [role].
Your task is to [goal].
Respond in [format].
Use the following context if available:
{context}
```

Example:

```
text
```

```
You are a helpful customer support assistant.

Your task is to answer questions related to refunds
and account access.

Respond only with direct, polite answers in JSON
format:

{

  "response": "your answer",

  "action": null

}
```

Common Prompt Patterns

Role Definition

Pattern Type Prompt Snippet

Friendly Bot "You are a helpful and friendly assistant."

Strict Analyst "You are a compliance-focused legal advisor."

Pattern Type Prompt Snippet

Task Agent   "Your only job is to summarize long documents."

Input Behavior Control

Behavior	Prompt Add-on
Reduce hallucination	"Only answer based on provided information."
Add fallback	"If you're unsure, say 'I don't know.'"
Clarify question	"Ask for clarification if the request is vague."
Be concise	"Respond in 2–3 short, direct sentences."

Tool Use Prompt Example

```text
```

```
You are a personal assistant.

When users ask for calendar help, use the tool
`create_event`.

Otherwise, answer normally.

Respond in JSON format.
```

Output Format Prompts

JSON Format

```text
```

```
Respond with a valid JSON object:

{
```

```
  "summary": "...",
  "action": "..."
}
```

Use this when:

Parsing agent output in code

Making agents trigger actions programmatically

Markdown Format

```
text
```

```
Please format your answer in markdown. Use bold for
headers and bullet points for lists.
```

Useful for:

Agents that output documentation, reports, or summaries in UI-rich environments.

Few-Shot Prompting Template

```
text
```

```
You are a financial analyst. Summarize quarterly
reports.


Example 1:

Input: "Q1 revenue up 12%..."

Output: "Positive revenue growth in Q1. Consider
reinvestment."
```

```
Example 2:

Input: "Q2 revenue dropped..."

Output: "Revenue declined. Monitor fixed costs."


Now summarize:

Input: {your_input_here}
```

Use this to:

Teach agent patterns or tone

Improve consistency in decision-heavy tasks

RAG Integration Prompt

```
text


You are a technical assistant. Use the documents
below to answer.


Context:
{retrieved_chunks}


User: {query}


If the answer is not in the documents, reply: "The
information is not available."
```

This keeps answers grounded and reduces hallucination.

Prompt Testing Tips

Technique	Benefit
Test in OpenAI Playground	See how model behaves before coding
Log and compare prompts	Track improvements and regressions
Save prompt versions	Version prompts like code
Refactor regularly	Prompt design evolves with user feedback

Memory-Ready Prompt Design

```
text
```

You remember previous tasks and conversations with the user.

Use past interactions to personalize your response.

Add when:

Memory is enabled

You want agents to personalize tone or reasoning

Final Checklist: Prompt Best Practices

Principle	Guideline
Clarity	Be explicit about the agent's role and scope
Format	Define exactly how the agent should respond
Control	Tell the agent what not to do (e.g., "Do not speculate")
Safety	Instruct to handle sensitive topics carefully
Flexibility	Allow fallback responses for edge cases

Summary

Strong prompts = strong agents. Use these proven patterns to design predictable, safe, and efficient agent behavior. Combine them with tools, memory, and RAG to build agents that respond like experts—consistently and clearly.

B.3 Deployment and Optimization Checklists

This cheat sheet gives you a **step-by-step guide to deploying, scaling, and optimizing** OpenAI Agent SDK projects for production. Whether you're preparing a cloud deployment, trimming cost, or hardening agent reliability—use these checklists to stay sharp and ship confidently.

Agent Deployment Checklist

Environment Setup

Environment variables configured (`OPENAI_API_KEY`, secrets)

Dockerfile or virtual environment defined

Dependencies locked (e.g., `requirements.txt`, `pip freeze`)

Dev and prod configs separated

Code & Project Structure

Modular agent creation function

Tool functions isolated and reusable

Configurable models (via `.env`, `config.py`, or JSON)

Logging implemented (file + stdout)

Deployment Targets

Supports local run and cloud deployment (e.g., FastAPI, Flask)

Compatible with serverless platforms (e.g., Vercel, AWS Lambda)

Container-ready (Docker build works)

Live test endpoint or CLI available

Security

API keys stored securely (not hardcoded)

Input validation and sanitation on all user inputs

Rate limiting or authentication enabled (if public-facing)

Error logs avoid exposing sensitive info

Performance Optimization Checklist

Prompt + Token Efficiency

Prompts are short, focused, and reusable

Instructions do not repeat unnecessarily

Output format is structured (e.g., JSON) to avoid verbosity

Prompt versions are tested for cost vs. quality

Model Selection

GPT-3.5 used for low-complexity tasks

GPT-4 Turbo or GPT-4o used for critical reasoning

Models evaluated for latency vs. accuracy

Tool & API Usage

Tools are only registered when needed

External API calls are cached or throttled

Function inputs are validated before execution

Retry logic included for flaky endpoints

Memory Management

Memory is summarized or trimmed when long

Retrieval (RAG) tuned for relevance + efficiency

Persistent memory storage (if required) is optimized (e.g., Redis, Supabase)

Observability & Monitoring Checklist

Logging

Input/output for every agent call is logged

Tool invocations are timestamped and stored

Errors and exceptions are clearly logged with tracebacks

Monitoring

Token usage tracked per call

Latency recorded per request

Failure rates tracked for tools and models

Testing & Evaluation

Unit tests written for tools and prompt formats

Agent test cases simulate real-world queries

Logs reviewed regularly for prompt drift or regressions

Cost Control Checklist

Strategy	Applied?
GPT-3.5 used for high-volume tasks	
Prompt size trimmed (<500 tokens)	
Outputs limited to essential fields	
Redundant memory/context removed	
Tool results cached where possible	
Logs include cost estimates	

Reliability + Fallbacks

Max iterations defined for agent loops

Output validation (e.g., `json.loads()` with retry)

Fallback responses for "I don't know" or invalid tool output

Human-in-the-loop enabled for sensitive flows (optional)

Summary

Use this checklist every time you:

Launch an agent to production

Optimize an existing deployment

Add new tools, memory, or workflows

It helps ensure your agent is **secure, scalable, and cost-effective**—ready for real-world usage.

Build it right once. Maintain it easily forever.

Appendix C: Resources for Continued Learning

C.1 Recommended Books, Tutorials, and Courses

To become an expert agent developer, you need to stay up to date with both **foundational knowledge** and **hands-on frameworks**. Below is a collection of **books, video tutorials, and courses** to help you sharpen your skills and deepen your understanding of autonomous agents, prompt engineering, RAG, and multi-agent systems.

Books

Title	Description
"Designing Agentive Technology" by Christopher Noessel	A non-technical but strategic look at how intelligent agents can be designed to assist humans.
"LangChain in Action" *(Early Access)*	Hands-on guide to LangChain, RAG, and agents using Python. Great for workflow orchestration and RAG with LLMs.
"Practical AI Agents" *(O'Reilly upcoming)*	A future-forward deep dive into building AI agents, including planning, memory, tool use, and collaboration.
"Architecting Large Language Model Applications" *(Microsoft eBook)*	Covers multi-agent systems, open-source stacks, and evaluation methods. Available free on Microsoft Learn.

Courses and Bootcamps

Platform	Course Name	Focus Area
DeepLearning.AI	ChatGPT Prompt Engineering	Prompting, function calling, structured output
LangChain	LangChain Courses	Tool use, agents, LangGraph, RAG
Full Stack Deep Learning	LLM Bootcamp	End-to-end LLM systems, agents, APIs
Microsoft Learn	AI Engineering Path	Azure OpenAI, SDKs, evaluation
Coursera	Building Generative AI Applications with LLMs	Industry use cases, agent deployment, model selection

Video Tutorials and YouTube Channels

Channel	Focus	Why Watch
Fireship	AI tools & dev stack s	Fast-paced, entertaining dev content
AI Explained	LLM use cases & breakdowns	Great for beginners and intermediate users
LangChain YouTube	LangGraph, agent demos	Official guides and case studies
AI Engineer (Swyx)	Agent architectures & trends	Deep dives into cutting-edge agent systems
AssemblyAI	LLMs, audio + multimodal agents	Tutorials with code and real-world examples

Web-Based Playgrounds and Labs

Tool	Description
OpenAI Playground	Test models, tools, and agents directly via browser
LangSmith	Debug, trace, and evaluate LLM apps
PromptLayer	Track and compare prompt performance
Replit AI Templates	Code-ready agent templates and prototypes

Bonus Learning Topics to Explore

Topic	Why It Matters
Retrieval-Augmented Generation (RAG)	Reduces hallucinations and grounds responses in real data

Topic	Why It Matters
Vector Databases (e.g., FAISS, Chroma)	Core to memory, document search, and context injection
Multi-Agent Frameworks (AutoGen, CrewAI)	Enable agent collaboration and planning
Guardrails & Evaluation (Guardrails AI, OpenAI Evals)	Help you enforce safety and measure output quality
Model Fine-Tuning (OpenAI, Hugging Face PEFT)	Customize agent behavior for specific industries or tones

Pro Tip: Build While You Learn

Learning agents is best done by building your own:

Create one new agent project per week (e.g., travel planner, report summarizer, Slack bot)

Use real data (PDFs, APIs, knowledge bases)

Share your learnings via blog posts or GitHub

Learning by doing is the fastest path to mastery in the agentic AI era.

C.2 Online Communities and Forums

Staying active in the right communities will help you **learn faster, get help when you're stuck**, and stay ahead of the curve in the fast-moving world of agent development. This section lists the most active and helpful online spaces for developers working with the **OpenAI Agents SDK**, multi-agent systems, and LLM-based apps.

OpenAI-Specific Communities

OpenAI Developer Forum

Purpose: Official forum for all things OpenAI

Why Join: Direct discussions on GPT-4, Agents SDK, API usage, and product updates

Bonus: OpenAI staff frequently respond to top questions

OpenAI GitHub Repos

Key Repos: `openai-python`, `openai-cookbook`, `openai/openai-agents`

Why Watch: SDK updates, bug reports, example projects

Tip: Star and "Watch" repos to get release notifications

LangChain + Agent Ecosystem

LangChain Discord

Purpose: Community hub for LangChain, LangGraph, and LangSmith

Channels: `#agents`, `#langgraph`, `#use-cases`, `#rag`, `#langsmith`

Why Join: Real-time help with chaining tools, memory, RAG, and workflows

---

CrewAI GitHub Discussions

Focus: Multi-agent collaboration framework built on OpenAI

Why Join: Share agent templates, get help building role-based teams of agents

Bonus: Actively maintained by the creator

AutoGen Discussions

Focus: Microsoft's framework for LLM agent collaboration

Why Join: Learn advanced agent planning and dialogue coordination

Great For: Building research assistants and multi-role workflows

---

General AI Dev & Engineering Forums

AI Engineers Community (Swyx)

Medium: Newsletter, podcast, Discord

Why Join: Deep technical breakdowns of agent architectures, production use cases

Audience: Serious LLM builders and startup engineers

[Twitter / X Hashtags & Threads]

Top Hashtags: #AIagents, #LLMops, #LangChain, #GPT4, #AutoGen

People to Follow:

@amasad (OpenAI VP of Product)

@swyx (AI engineer and educator)

@yoheinakajima (AutoGPT pioneer)

Use these to stay current with new frameworks, demos, and research drops.

Reddit – r/LocalLLaMA, r/LanguageTechnology, r/MachineLearning

Why Useful: Discussions on fine-tuning, local agents, LLM use cases

Tip: Use Reddit to compare community insights across platforms and frameworks

---

YouTube + Live Learning

Channel	Why Follow
LangChain YouTube	Tutorials, LangGraph, LangSmith guides

Channel	Why Follow
AI Explained	Breakdown of agent behavior and tools
Fireship	Quick s of AI dev stacks
AssemblyAI	Great for multimodal + agent tutorials

How to Make the Most of These Communities

Action	Benefit
Ask specific questions	Get fast, focused answers
Share your projects	Receive feedback and recognition
Help others	Reinforce your own learning
Bookmark useful threads	Build your own agent knowledge base
Stay active weekly	Stay current with updates and trends

Don't build in isolation.
Join the conversation, learn from others, and grow your skillset faster.

Being part of these communities is how you'll move from beginner to expert—and potentially even contribute back to the tools shaping the future of AI.

C.3 Useful GitHub Repositories

This section provides a list of **must-follow GitHub repositories** that are relevant to developers working with the **OpenAI Agents SDK**, agent frameworks, multi-agent systems, tool integrations, and real-world deployments. These open-source projects offer examples, utilities, and building blocks for production-ready agents.

Core OpenAI Repos

◆ **openai/openai-python**

The official OpenAI Python SDK.

Includes support for GPT models, function calling, and Agents SDK.

Frequently updated with new API features and usage examples.

◆ **openai/openai-cookbook**

Practical guides and code examples for using OpenAI APIs effectively.

Covers prompting, function calling, fine-tuning, and evaluation.

Great for learning best practices through working code.

Tooling and Frameworks for Agents

◆ **langchain-ai/langchain**

Modular framework for LLM applications, agents, and RAG.

Offers chains, memory modules, tools, and integrations.

Core for anyone building advanced agent systems.

◆ **langchain-ai/langgraph**

Stateful, multi-agent workflow orchestration powered by LangChain.

Visual and programmable graph-based control over agent logic.

Ideal for complex decision trees and parallel agent workflows.

◆ **joaomdmoura/crewai**

Framework for building multi-agent systems with specialized roles.

Focuses on team-based agents that collaborate.

Great starting point for building planning/research-oriented systems.

◆ microsoft/autogen

Framework for collaborative agent workflows and self-reflection loops.

Includes smart agent planning, multi-agent chat, and tool orchestration.

Used for code generation, research assistants, and team agents.

◆ guardrails-ai/guardrails

Validates and enforces structure, safety, and reliability in LLM outputs.

Ensures output conforms to formats (e.g., JSON, XML).

Integrates with OpenAI, LangChain, and Hugging Face.

Developer Utilities and Demos

◆ prompt-engineering/prompt-patterns

Collection of reusable prompt patterns for various tasks.

Helps you quickly build effective prompts for agents and tools.

Covers formatting, decision-making, summarization, and more.

◆ promptslab/Promptify

Fast prototyping library for prompt engineering and tool usage.

Great for lightweight LLM experiments and testing prompt behaviors.

◆ mshumer/gpt-4-agent

Open-source GPT-4 agent architecture from scratch.

Shows how to build a fully functioning autonomous agent.

Easy to fork, extend, and customize.

☐ Experimentation and RAG Projects

◆ hwchase17/langchainhub

Community-driven collection of LangChain agent examples and templates.

Covers tasks like document QA, assistant bots, and RAG pipelines.

◆ lucidrains/PaLM-rlhf-pytorch

Reinforcement learning fine-tuning for LLMs (advanced).

Useful for advanced users looking to train agents with feedback.

◆ LangChainAI/langsmith

Logging, tracing, and evaluation framework for LLM workflows.

Essential for debugging, testing, and improving agent behavior.

Tips for Using These Repos

Strategy	Benefit
Star + Watch repos	Stay notified on updates
Read Issues and Discussions	Learn from real-world problems
Clone + run quick demos	Learn through execution
Fork and customize for your needs	Build on top of working foundations
Compare implementation patterns	See how other devs structure workflows

---

Summary

These GitHub repositories provide **real-world code**, battle-tested components, and active communities to help you build better agents, faster. Bookmark this list, follow the ones you use most, and consider contributing to the ecosystem as you grow.

Appendix D: Glossary of Key Terms

D.1 Comprehensive Definitions of Technical Terms

This glossary defines key technical terms and concepts used throughout this book to ensure clarity and consistency. Use it as a quick reference for revisiting important ideas as you build with the OpenAI Agents SDK.

Agent (AI Agent)

An autonomous software entity that can understand input, reason through decisions, and take action—usually powered by a language model like GPT-4.

Agent Lifecycle

The stages an agent goes through, including initialization, context setup, tool usage, response generation, and termination.

Agents SDK

A toolkit provided by OpenAI to build and manage AI agents using their language models, tools (functions), and memory features.

API (Application Programming Interface)

A defined way for one program or service to interact with another. Agents often use APIs to retrieve external data or trigger actions.

Authentication

The process of verifying identity—typically with an API key—to gain access to a system or resource like the OpenAI API.

Autonomous Workflow

A sequence of steps that an agent or group of agents completes automatically, without human intervention.

Context Window

The maximum number of tokens (words or characters) a language model can consider at once. GPT-4 Turbo supports up to 128k tokens.

Few-Shot Prompting

A prompting strategy where a few examples are provided to teach the model how to respond.

Fine-Tuning

Training a pre-trained model on new data to specialize its behavior for a specific domain or task.

Function Calling

The mechanism that allows an LLM to trigger predefined tools (functions) with structured input/output.

GPT-4 / GPT-4 Turbo / GPT-4o

OpenAI's advanced language models. GPT-4o is the most recent, offering multimodal input/output with better speed and cost efficiency.

Guardrails

Safety mechanisms that constrain agent behavior to prevent harmful, biased, or invalid outputs.

Hallucination

When a model generates output that is plausible-sounding but factually incorrect or unsupported.

JSON (JavaScript Object Notation)

A structured data format commonly used for APIs and agent responses. It allows easy parsing and validation.

LangChain

A framework for building applications with LLMs using chains, memory, tools, and agents.

LangGraph

A graph-based framework for orchestrating stateful, multi-agent workflows using LangChain components.

Memory (in Agents)

Persistent or session-based storage of context that agents can recall in future interactions.

Model

A machine learning system (like GPT-4) that processes input and generates intelligent output. Also referred to as an LLM.

Multi-Agent System

A coordinated group of agents working together to complete complex tasks through communication and delegation.

Prompt

The input or instruction given to a language model to guide its response. Can include system, user, and function messages.

Prompt Engineering

The craft of designing effective prompts to control model behavior and produce useful output.

RAG (Retrieval-Augmented Generation)

A technique that retrieves relevant data (e.g., from a database or documents) to ground a language model's response in real facts.

Rate Limit

A restriction on how many API calls can be made per minute/hour, based on your usage tier or plan.

Tool (in Agents SDK)

A callable function that agents can use to perform tasks, fetch data, or interact with external systems.

Token

A unit of text (word fragment, word, or character). Models have token limits, which affect how much input/output they can process.

Validation

The process of checking whether the output (e.g., JSON) or function input is correctly structured or meets expectations.

Workflow (Agentic)

A sequence of steps or logic that an agent follows to complete a task—can be linear, conditional, or multi-agent.

Tip

As the OpenAI Agents SDK evolves, always check the official docs for updated terminology and behaviors: https://platform.openai.com/docs/agents

OpenAI Agents SDK: A Hands-On Guide to Building Autonomous Agents with OpenAI's Language Models

Chapter 1: Introduction to OpenAI Agents SDK

1.1 What are Autonomous AI Agents?

1.2 of OpenAI Agents SDK

1.3 Key Features and Capabilities

1.4 Real-world Applications

1.5 Audience and Prerequisites

1.6 How to Use This Book Effectively

Chapter 2: Setting Up Your Development Environment

2.1 Installation and Requirements

2.2 SDK Installation (Local and Cloud Environments)

2.3 API Keys and Authentication

6.5 Practical Project: Autonomous Data Analyst Agent

Chapter 7: Designing and Managing Autonomous Workflows

7.1 Autonomous Workflow Fundamentals

7.2 Designing Sequential and Parallel Workflows

7.3 Handling Workflow Errors and Exceptions

7.4 Monitoring and Observability

7.5 Project: Autonomous Marketing Automation Agent

Chapter 8: Optimizing, Deploying, and Scaling Your Agents

8.1 Optimization for Cost and Efficiency

8.2 Debugging and Performance Monitoring in Production

8.3 Deployment Options (Docker, Kubernetes, Cloud Platforms)

8.4 Best Practices for Scaling Autonomous Agents

8.5 Maintaining Your Agents in Production

Chapter 9: Security, Ethics, and Regulatory Compliance

9.1 Ensuring Agent Security

9.2 Managing Sensitive Information

9.3 Ethical Considerations for Autonomous Agents

9.4 Compliance with Regulations (GDPR, HIPAA)

9.5 Mitigating Bias and Promoting Responsible AI

Chapter 10: Real-World Case Studies

10.1 Case Study: Enterprise Customer Support Automation

10.2 Case Study: Automated Content Generation System

10.3 Case Study: Financial Advisory and Decision-making Agent

10.4 Case Study: Autonomous Research Assistant

10.5 Key Lessons and Industry Insights

Chapter 11: Advanced Topics and Emerging Trends

11.1 Fine-Tuning Models for Custom Agents

11.2 Leveraging Retrieval-Augmented Generation (RAG)

11.3 Multi-agent Swarm Systems

11.4 Strategic Decision-making and Predictive Agents

11.5 Integrating with LangChain, LangGraph, AutoGen, and CrewAI

11.6 Exploring the Future of Autonomous AI Agents

Chapter 12: Troubleshooting and Common Challenges

12.1 Identifying Common Issues

12.2 Debugging Tools and Techniques

12.3 Managing Unexpected Agent Behaviors

12.4 Resolving Performance Bottlenecks

12.5 FAQs and Quick Solutions Guide

Chapter 13: Conclusion and Next Steps

13.1 Summary of Key Learnings

13.2 Continuous Learning Resources and Next Steps

13.3 Staying Updated with Industry Trends

13.4 Final Recommendations for Building Successful Agents

Appendices

Appendix A: OpenAI Agents SDK Complete Reference

A.1 SDK Functions and Classes

A.2 SDK Error Codes and Troubleshooting

Appendix B: Quickstart Templates and Cheat Sheets

B.1 Agent Project Templates

B.2 Prompt Engineering Cheat Sheets

cc

Appendix C: Resources for Continued Learning

C.1 Recommended Books, Tutorials, and Courses

C.2 Online Communities and Forums

C.3 Useful GitHub Repositories

Appendix D: Glossary of Key Terms

D.1 Comprehensive Definitions of Technical Terms

This clearly structured **Table of Contents** ensures the book is comprehensive, practical, logically progressive, and designed explicitly to deliver outstanding value to readers.

If you have additional refinements or adjustments, let me know!

4.5